9.0/8

*God*

# Learning of God

Christian Jr./Sr. High School
2100 Greenfield Dr
El Cajon, CA 92019

## Readings from
## Amy Carmichael

### Compiled by Stuart & Brenda Blanch

CHRISTIAN • LITERATURE • CRUSADE
Fort Washington, Pennsylvania 19034

*CHRISTIAN LITERATURE CRUSADE*
*U.S.A.*
P.O. Box 1449, Fort Washington, PA 19034

*GREAT BRITAIN*
51 The Dean, Alresford, Hants. SO24 9BJ

*AUSTRALIA*
P.O. Box 419M, Manunda, QLD 4879

*NEW ZEALAND*
10 MacArthur Street, Feilding

*ISBN 0-87508-086-3*

*Printed in the United States of America*

# Contents

# Key to Extracts

The letters following each extract refer to the work from which it is taken. Figures represent page numbers.

# Amy Carmichael and the Dohnavur Fellowship

Amy Carmichael was born at Millisle, in County Down, Northern Ireland, on December 16th 1867.

Early in her life she was challenged by the needs of the under-privileged, and in her late teens taught boys of Belfast in a night school, and ran a Bible class for mill girls. She then had a spell of working in the slums of Manchester, and lived very near the poverty line herself. Illness led to her being unofficially adopted as daughter, in place of the daughter he had lost, by an old friend of the family, Mr Robert Wilson, who was at that time chairman of the Keswick Convention.

At the age of twenty-six, strongly convinced of a missionary call, Amy sailed for Japan. Fifteen months of crowded life and many remarkable experiences followed, before she became ill again and had to return to England.

In 1895 an opportunity to go to India presented itself. This she eagerly accepted, and never again returned to Britain.

After a period of language study she began touring the villages of the Tirunelveli District in Madras State (now Tamil Nadu) with a group of Indian Christian women. She and her companions made a big impact on the countryside with their teaching and example.

Then in 1901 a seven-year-old child, who had run away from a Hindu temple, was brought to Amy. This incident resulted in the discovery, by patient enquiry and research, of the Devadasi system by which baby girls could be dedicated to Hindu temples to become 'servants of the gods'. These Devadasis inevitably had to serve as cult prostitutes. Amy was convinced that God had brought these facts to light in order that she should rescue and make a home for children who for this, or any other reason were in danger of immoral exploitation.

The British administration did nothing to stop the practice of dedicating little children to Hindu temples; but after India became independent in 1947, it was prohibited by Act of Parliament.

To begin with it was hard to find these endangered children, and those who were rescued were often delicate and hard to rear. Amy — 'Amma', as she came to be called — was criticized, too, for leaving her successful village evangelism to 'become a nursemaid', and the champion of a lost cause. But she saw her babies as the missionaries of the future, and so persisted in spite of discouragement.

From the beginning of her missionary career Amma had done a lot of writing and her books had a wide circulation. Soon people all over the Christian world were reading about and praying for the children of India, and especially for Amma's family in Dohnavur. As years passed she was joined in her work by men and women from various countries, and so the Dohnavur Fellowship came into being. Its aims and principles are best explained in her own words, written in the late 1930s:

> From the first we thought of the children as our own. We did not make a Home for them; when they came to us they were at home. And so from the beginning we were a family, never an institution; and we all, Indian and European, men and women, live and work together on the lines of an Indian family, each contributing what each has to offer for the help of all. We have no salaried workers, Indian or foreign; make no appeal for funds; and authorize none to be made for us. We have never lacked. As the needs grew supplies came; and as we advance we find that our Unseen Leader is moving on before us. There are between six and seven hundred in the family, several outposts in the villages and medical work.

When the Family had become well established and Fellowship

members had brought many skills to it, a chance visitor seeing the pleasant cottage homes around the House of Prayer (church), the schools, workshops, weaving sheds, sewing-rooms, offices and the farm with its rice land, fruit and vegetable gardens and dairy herd, the book-room and the hospital, might have thought that he had stumbled upon an experiment in community living in a model village. It was always more than this. Character training was paramount, and the needs of the Christless villages around were never forgotten. The aim was always to demonstrate God's love in action as well as by teaching. The hospital, staffed by grown-up children of the Family, has always been in the forefront of its outreach.

In 1932 Amma had an accident, and until her death in 1951 was virtually house-bound. She remained closely in touch with the Family and its affairs until almost the end, and was surprisingly aware also of world events. She wrote extensively in those years and exercised a wide influence.

Indian independence, and legislation about the temple children and other social matters, brought many changes to the work of the Fellowship, as did Amma's gradual withdrawal from responsibility. It became clear to leading members of the Fellowship after independence that the education and vocational training of the children and young people needed a different context from that of private missionary enterprise. They began to go to government-recognized Christian high schools outside Dohnavur for the last years of their education and then to various training institutions or colleges. Amma gave her blessing to these changes. All who could make the grade were encouraged to find employment, and only to return to Dohnavur to work if convinced of God's call to do so. The Family now (in 1985) numbers nearly five hundred.

The policy of accepting children only if they have no family to care for them was adhered to, and most of those who come now are the victims of broken marriages or other domestic tragedies. Dohnavur is still their only home. They return for holidays and in any crisis usually turn to the Fellowship for help and advice. Many of the Old Boys and Old Girls are in fact missionaries to their own people as they work all over India as teachers, nurses, technicians, clerks, accountants, wardens and matrons, church workers of different kinds and in many other professions. Amma's hope is also being fulfilled as the leadership of the Fellowship is now predominantly Indian — and the Lord whom Amma loved so much is still the Unseen Leader over all.

# Introduction by Bishop Stuart Blanch

I owe it to my wife that I first became acquainted with Amy Carmichael and with the Dohnavur Fellowship. She had encountered in this country people who were familiar with the work of Amy Carmichael, and wrote to me when I was serving in the RAF in India during the war suggesting that if I ever should have leave I should visit Dohnavur.

I did not react all that favourably to the suggestion. Tirunelveli was hundreds of miles from my home base and in any case service men, when the questions of leave arose, turned instinctively to the thought of cool days and heady nights in the mountain resort of Darjeeling. But we all 'learn from God'. When I had the offer of a month's leave I remembered my wife's letter and wrote to Dohnavur inviting myself to a holiday there. I received a warm and welcoming letter. Yes, it was hundreds of miles away but I was a member of aircrew and it ought not to be too difficult to cadge a lift to Madras and to travel on from there by train.

So it was that I was met at the nearest station, and had my first glimpse of the mission compound to which I was committed for the next month. It was reassuring; it stood in a hot, sandy plain but the compound itself was a green oasis, well supplied with grass and trees and shade. The buildings presented a harmonious combination of Indian and Chinese styles, and it altogether lacked that dismal institutional aspect which so often characterises establishments of this kind. Moreover, I was conducted to a small, but by RAF standards, lavish little bungalow with a bedroom, a primitive bathroom, and a large verandah, within a group of trees. I was wholeheartedly welcomed by the Community who were no doubt a little puzzled as to why this young man had taken the trouble to travel all the way on his own from Barrackpore, near Calcutta, to spend his leave with them.

I ask myself now — over forty years later — why I really went, what I expected, and how I proposed to spend my time. I had only comparatively recently become a practising Christian, and I was already an enthusiastic student of the Bible, relying on a series of Bible Reading Fellowship notes which I had brought with me from England. But otherwise I probably needed the time to consider the long-term implications of my new-found relationship with Christ. Time was not difficult to find under the conditions in which I was now living. But once a day I used to desert my books and climb the tower to a room reserved for prayer overlooking the majestic mountains to the west, with the sun setting over them.

There were other activities in which I could be engaged. I habitually attended the Community worship in which the children joined — worship which was imaginatively adapted to the Indian temperament, far removed from the stately cadences of the Book of Common Prayer. I accompanied the doctor to the leprosy clinic on the compound, and I had my first experience — apart from the streets of Calcutta — of seeing the physical and mental ravages of this dreaded disease on those who came from the countryside around to receive treatment. I accompanied the farm manager on his occasional forays into the Indian farming community around Dohnavur. I observed the interminable negotiations in which the farm manager was involved, and had — as a matter of courtesy — to drink more coconut milk than was good for me. I accompanied other members of the Community on evangelistic visits in the neighbouring villages and was deeply impressed by the friendly reception which they received. For part of the time I went to the so-called 'forest houses' designed as a relief from the torrid heat of the summer months on the plain. It proved to be a long walk and in some places a steep climb along the paths to the three thousand feet above sea level, where little holiday chalets had been constructed.

It was worth the walk and the climb; there were cool rock-pools to swim in; the trees round our humble habitations were full of monkeys chattering amongst themselves, complaining about us, always ready to sweep down and steal the food from the tables. And there was the jungle, and the stealthy noise of mountain animals as they nosed around the apparently flimsy walls within which we slept.

The most striking feature, however, of Dohnavur was not the buildings, or the farm, or the mountain houses, but the joyful sound of children at work and at play in, as it seemed, every nook and cranny. There were hundreds of them, of varying ages. Most had been destined to become 'servants of the gods' in Hindu temples — a practice since outlawed by the Indian government. None had parents or other relatives who were able or willing to care for them, and almost all had been in danger of being exploited for immoral purposes before coming to Dohnavur. Their clothes were bright, the classrooms were colourful, and everywhere, for all the difficulties of any such undertaking, was the sense of a total Christian community at work and at play and at worship.

Amy Carmichael was the invisible but palpable presence throughout the Community. She was confined to her room, but what she was learning from God herself she was daily communicating to the other members of the Fellowship through messages to them, combined with telling comments on Holy Scripture and quotations from her most recent reading. So in a sense I knew her long before I actually met her towards the end of my stay when I was invited to spend a few minutes with her in her room. Perhaps she too was a little puzzled as to why I had come and what I had been doing over the past month. But she was gracious enough not to ask either of these questions. She spoke to me about my wife and my home and about my life in the Air Force. She was a person chastened by suffering, who nevertheless radiated peace and joy. I 'took knowledge of her that she had been with Jesus'. So this was the remarkable woman, reared in Irish Protestantism, an intrepid traveller, a doughty warrior against the abuses of children, and the founder of a Fellowship which exists to this day and owes its character to her.

Amy Carmichael's achievements were not of such a kind as to command a world-wide press. She would not have attracted busy journalists or television crews to her door — neither would she have wished to do so; it was essential for the work that it should be done in secret. She did not cry or lift up her voice in the street; she did not appeal for money. It was largely a hidden ministry, first of all to deprived and threatened children, subsequently to the community around her and ultimately to friends and associates of Dohnavur throughout the world. What she was 'learning from God' she was communicating along hidden channels to many souls also eager to learn from God.

But there was one feature of her ministry which would be remarkable now and was even more remarkable in her own day. She was brought up a Presbyterian, and an Irish one at that, conditioned no doubt by the family environment to look askance at any deviation from the astringent faith of her fathers, suspicious, no doubt, of Catholic models, so distinct as they seemed from the pure truth of the gospel. As these readings will reveal she found a precious affinity with Christian souls of every age in the life of the Church, from whom she was otherwise markedly divided by formidable doctrinal barriers. This had all the appearance of being accidental; she was always 'learning from God' but she was equally ready to learn from a variety of books which her friends sent her from England. As you will observe, those books constituted a 'catholic' collection. It was not that she used them as her guides, but that, having learned from God herself, she found a strange and surprising affinity with these writers who — so it would seem — floated inconsequentially into her orbit. In her heart there was, as it were, a cry of recognition: 'It is the Lord!' — whether He be identified in a Protestant conventicle, in a continental monastry, or in the luxuriant growth of a Post-Tridentine spiritual tradition. It was by a miraculous alchemy that all these seemingly varied experiences of the living God combined in the hidden life of a largely unknown woman, confined to her room in a distant dependency of the British Empire. This is what makes her writings a steady source of inspiration to men and women of the western world who have never met her, have never visited India, and perhaps have little knowledge of how the Dohnavur Fellowship started.

I hope that this anthology, for which I may say my wife has been entirely responsible, will find its way into the hands of some at least who will be reading Amy Carmichael's words for the first time, and will discover in them — as both my wife and I have done — a deep solace for the spirit and a renewed hope for the unity of the Christian Church. Whilst the great Christian institutions grope laboriously for a formula on which a new unity can be created, there are those who, whilst still divided by dogmatic and institutional barriers, find amongst themselves a deep understanding and sympathy arising out of devotion to the one Lord and to the one Church.

My wife and I would like to express our gratitude to the SPCK and in particular to Myrtle Powley who provided the ample material on which this anthology is based, and has guided us with a sure touch to the completion of that which she initially suggested. We would like also to express our appreciation to the Dohnavur Fellowship for their warm and friendly welcome when in 1979 my wife and I were able to visit Dohnavur for the first time together.

# 1867 — 1901

The readings in this section relate to the
early period of the life of Amy Carmichael ('Amma'),
when she was learning from God certain lessons
which were to be of great importance in the
founding of the work at Dohnavur.

Born in 1867 in Northern Ireland, she was in
her early twenties when she received her missionary call.
After little more than a year in Japan,
she returned briefly to Britain before
sailing in late 1895 for India, where she
remained until her death in 1951.

## Make Me Thy Fuel

From prayer that asks that I may be
Sheltered from winds that beat on Thee,
From fearing when I should aspire,
From faltering when I should climb higher,
From silken self, O Captain, free
Thy soldier who would follow Thee.

From subtle love of softening things,
From easy choices, weakenings,
Not thus are spirits fortified,
Not this way went the Crucified,
From all that dims Thy Calvary,
O Lamb of God, deliver me.

Give me the love that leads the way,
The faith that nothing can dismay,
The hope no disappointments tire,
The passion that will burn like fire,
Let me not sink to be a clod:
Make me Thy fuel, Flame of God.

TJ 94

### An early memory

My first memory as a tiny child is this: after the nursery light had been turned low and I was quite alone, I used to smooth a little place on the sheet, and say aloud, but softly, to our Father, 'Please come and sit with me.' And that baby custom left something which recurs and is with me still. *Our God is a God at hand,* and 'To Him who is everywhere, men come not by travelling but by loving.'

RB 196

### 'If any man's work abide . . .'

It was a dull Sunday morning in a street in Belfast . . . My brothers and sisters and I were returning with our mother from church when we met a poor, pathetic old woman who was carrying a heavy bundle. We had never seen such a thing in Presbyterian Belfast on Sunday, and, moved by sudden pity, my brothers and I turned with her, relieved her of the bundle, took her by her arms as though they had been handles, and helped her along. This meant facing all the respectable people who were, like ourselves, on their way home. It was a horrid moment. We were only two boys and a girl, and not at all exalted Christians. We hated doing it. Crimson all over (at least we felt crimson, soul and body of us) we plodded on, a wet wind blowing us about, and blowing, too, the rags of that poor old woman, till she seemed like a bundle of feathers and we unhappily mixed up with them. But just as we passed a fountain, recently built near the kerbstone, this mighty phrase was suddenly flashed as it were through the grey drizzle: *'Gold, silver, precious stones, wood, hay, stubble — every man's work shall be made manifest; for the day shall declare it, because it shall be declared by fire; and the fire shall try every man's work of what sort it is. If any man's work abide —'*

*If any man's work abide:* I turned to see the voice that spoke

3

with me. The fountain, the muddy street, the people with their politely surprised faces, all this I saw, but saw nothing else. The blinding flash had come and gone; the ordinary was all about us. We went on. I said nothing to anyone, but I knew that something had happened that had changed life's values. Nothing could ever matter again but the things that were eternal.

GC 2

I am very grateful to my father for teaching me never to give in to a difficulty. . . . Fanny, my pony, did startling things if anything frightened her. I found that to sing softly in her ear soothed her. He taught me . . . how to ride with a light rein, and yet never lose control, and he taught me never to nag. All this came in useful long afterwards, for in some ways people are rather like ponies.

ACD 8

Near the end of my three years at school the CSSM held a Mission in Harrogate. My mother had often talked to me about the Lord Jesus, and often, as I sat on her knee, with her arms about me while she sang, 'Jesus, the very thought of Thee' and 'It passeth knowledge, that dear love of Thine', I had felt the love of the Lord Jesus, and, as it were, nestled in His love, just as I nestled in her arms. But I had not understood that there was something more to do, something that may be called coming to Him, or opening the door to Him, or giving oneself to Him.

I don't remember what the speaker spoke about, but after his address he told us to sing 'Jesus loves me, this I know', and then to be quiet. During those quiet few minutes, in His great mercy the Good Shepherd answered the prayers of my mother and father and many other loving ones, and drew me, even me, into His fold.

Afterwards when I began to understand more of what all this meant I found words which satisfied me. I do not know who wrote them:

> Upon a life I did not live,
> Upon a death I did not die,
> Another's life, Another's death,
> I stake my whole eternity.

ACD 17


## A lesson learned

*[One of the first lessons that the staunch Presbyterian had to learn was, as she said]:*

' . . . *to drop labels,* and to think only of the one true invisible Church, to which all who truly love the Lord belong. Suppose He came tomorrow, what would labels matter? I could almost see them dropping off as those who were waiting for their Lord rose in the air to meet Him. They would never think of them then, why think much of them now? . . . I grew to value the quietness of the Friends' way of worship, and also to care very much for the beauty of the Church of England ways.

ACD 37


## The same sword

When I was a little child I used to wish I could touch something that our Lord Jesus touched, or see something that He saw. Then suddenly to my delight I thought, But I *can* see something that He saw. He saw the very same moon and stars that I see. And I used to look at the moon and think, He saw you, He saw those funny marks in your face we call the man in the moon.

5

He looked up to you just as I look up at you tonight. Years afterwards someone gave me a bit of brick and a little slab of marble from Rome. It was wonderful to touch one of them and think, Perhaps the Apostle Paul or one of the martyrs touched this as they passed. But how much more wonderful is it to think that we have, for our own use, the very same sword our Lord used when the devil attacked him. Westcott says 'the word of God' in Ephesians 6.17 means 'a definite utterance of God'. We know these 'definite utterances' — we have the same Book that He had, and we can do as He did. So let us learn the 'definite utterances' that they may be ready in our minds: ready for use at the moment of need — our sword which never grows dull and rusty, but is always keen and bright. So once more I say, let us not expect defeat but victory. Let us take fast hold and keep fast hold of our sword, and we shall win in any assault of the enemy. The Lord quicken our expectation.

EW 39

### The hand behind the pattern

'When heaven is about to confer a great office on a man it always first exercises his mind and soul with suffering, and his body to hunger, and exposes him to extreme poverty, and baffles all his undertakings. By these means it stimulates his mind, hardens his nature, and enables him to do acts otherwise not possible to him,' wrote Mencius, the Chinese sage, two thousand years ago; and the illustration of the Chladni plate beautifully shows how these agitating circumstances can be caused to work together. You sprinkle sand on a brass plate fixed on a pedestal, and draw a bow across the edge of the plate, touching it at the same time with two fingers. Then, because of this touch, the sand does not fall into confusion but into an ordered pattern like music made visible. Each little grain of sand finds its place in that pattern. Not one grain is forgotten and left to drift about unregarded.

There is nothing in the vibrations of the bow to make a pattern. Suffering, hunger, poverty, baffling circumstances cannot of themselves make anything but confusion. But if there be the touch of the Hand, all these things work together for good, not for ill, not for discord, but for something like the harmony of music.

GM 39

### *Wilt Love Me? Trust Me? Praise Me?*

O thou belovèd child of My desire,
Whether I lead thee through green valleys,
      By still waters,
      Or through fire,
Or lay thee down in silence under snow,
Through any weather, and whatever
      Cloud may gather,
      Wind may blow —

Wilt love Me? trust Me? praise Me?

No gallant bird, O dearest Lord, am I,
That anywhere, in any weather,
      Rising singeth;
      Low I lie.
And yet I cannot fear, for I shall soar,
Thy love shall wing me, blessed Saviour;
      So I answer,
      I adore,
I love Thee, trust Thee, praise Thee.

TJ 10

8

## Early life in India

[*circa 1897*]  We were an itinerating band, furnished with a flag made of folds of black, red, white and yellow sateen, a most useful text for an impromptu sermon; and we found Eastern musical instruments useful too. Being the first women's band of its kind in the district, we walked circumspectly. I used to feel like a cat on the top of a wall — the sort of wall that is plentifully set with bits of broken bottles . . . Much of our time we spent in scouring the country round our different camping-places. Off we would go in the early morning, walking, or by bullock-cart, as many of us as could get in, packed under its curved mat roof. Stuffiness, weariness, that appalling sensation of almost sea-sickness which never forgets to afflict those naturally inclined thereto, all these disagreeables have faded, and one only remembers the loveliness of the early lights on palm and water and emerald sheet of rice-field; the songs by which we refreshed ourselves as we tumbled along in the heat; the pause outside the village we were to enter; the swift prayer for an open door; the entrance, all of us watching eagerly for signs of a welcome anywhere — for this was pioneer work, not work in prepared ground, and in scores of the places to which we went no white woman had ever been seen before.

Sometimes we would get out at the entrance of the village and walk on till we saw a friendly face — and we almost always found one. We usually separated then, and went two and two, and won our way past the men who would be sauntering in the front courtyard, and so penetrated to the women's rooms; or if that proved impossible, we held an open-air meeting somewhere; or sat down wherever we could and waited till someone came to talk, for we found — at festivals, for example — that if we waited in some quiet by-street, sitting apparently unconcerned, Indian guru-fashion, on a deserted verandah, or under a tree, that one by one people discovered us, and came and squatted down beside us and asked questions. Before the heat grew too intolerable we went home; and after breakfast, through the hottest hours, we had what would now be described as a Study Circle. . . .

The afternoons and evenings of those years were spent much as the mornings, except that we often joined the other side of the house in its avocations, and when missions to Christians were the order of the day, took our share in them. Sometimes we all went street-preaching together, with a baby organ by way of attraction; and Ponnammal soon developed a gift of fine and forceful speech, and could hold a turbulent open-air meeting in a big, busy market as easily as the decorous assembly settled in tidy rows in prayer-room or village church. So she was an immense help. Coming home, especially if the afternoon had been spent in some unresponsive village and we were feeling low, we used to sing the happiest things we knew.

Once, for a period which seemed ages long, we were shut out of the homes of the people, because some of them had believed our report. When we went to the villages where this had happened, we were pelted with ashes and rotten garlands from the necks of the idols. One day a great crowd drew round us and shouted its sentiments and made a most unholy racket. We stood under a burning sun till we were too tired to stand any longer; then as there was nothing else to be done, we knelt down in the middle of the rabble and prayed for it, after which it let us go. Once we were tom-tomed out of a village, accompanied by all the ragamuffins of the place — a new experience for Ponnammal; but she walked out of that village, I remember, with the utmost dignity, in nowise disturbed thereby. To those to whom such episodes sound rather extraordinary, and to whom the militant attitude is all wrong, I can only say that with the best intentions, as I think ours were, to live a peaceable life, we were never able to discover a way by which the captives of the devil could be delivered without offending that person. When doors lie open year after year, it only means that nothing vital has been done behind them. But open doors are such nice things that we were at first much troubled when they shut; it was then we comforted ourselves with song. And as opposition in one place usually led to blessing in another, we learned not to be moved from our purpose by talk about the unwisdom of shutting doors.

P 12

## Night in the East

Who can forget the first nights in the East? There is the night of velvet depths when the stars burn in ordered distances, one beyond the other for ever and for ever. And there is the night when the sky, lit with a little moon, is asleep in gauzy blue and the constellations appear in bright groups; and again there are full-moon nights, when every colour of the earth shows clear (only most strangely holy) and you feel it ungrateful to go to sleep while the very trees stand awake and conscious and worshipful.

RSP 66

## Itinerant missionary work

We went on that day to a village where they had listened splendidly only a week before. They had not time, it was a busy season. Then to a town, farther on, but it was quite impracticable. So we went to our friend the dear old Evangelist there, the blind old man. He and his wife are lights in that dark town. It is so refreshing to spend half an hour with two genuine good old Christians after a tug of war with the heathen; they have no idea they are helping you, but they are, and you return home ever so much happier for the sight of them.

As we came home we were almost mobbed. In the old days mobs there were of common occurence. It is a rough market town, and the people, after the first converts came, used to hoot us through the streets, and throw handfuls of sand at us, and shower ashes on our hair. In theory I like this very much, but in practice not at all. The yellings of the crowd, men chiefly, are not polite; the yelpings of the dogs, set on by sympathetic spectators; the sickening blaze of the sun and the reflected glare from the houses; the blinding dust in your eyes, and the queer feel of ashes down your neck; above all, the

12

sense that this sort of thing does no manner of good — all this row and all these feelings, one on top of the other, combine to make mobbing less interesting than might be expected. You hold on, and look up for patience, and good nature, and such like common graces, and you pray that you may not be down with fever tomorrow — for fever has a way of stopping work — and you get out of it all as quickly as you can without showing undue hurry. And then, though little they know it, you go and get a fresh baptism of love for them all.

TTA 196

## Happiness

In India the eyes which watch us are not deceived. They look through what is shown to what is. They are quick to detect tinsel. It is gold they seek. Happiness, especially the kind which does not depend upon circumstances, is gold. The golden quality of such happiness attracts and holds as nothing else does, for it is love made manifest. The 'happyfying' love of God, that which made men say of St. Anthony, 'He seemed to bear on his face, somehow or other, a gladness of Heaven that came from no human source.' That is gold.

TMS 174

## A testing of faith

In one of the houses we are passing, some years ago a boy was confined and guarded night and day. He was beaten hard; drugs were mixed with his food. When he slept, Vishnu's mark was put on his forehead, and the filthy water called holy, in which the idols had been washed, was sprinkled upon him. He was treated as an idiot, and a green paste, supposed to cure the insane, was rubbed upon his head. One night his father in great wrath took a knife, intending to stab him. 'I simply told

13

him,' said the boy, 'the words of our Master, "Fear not them that kill the body." ' Others interfered then, and withheld the father from killing his son. Violence having failed, it was proposed that a famous magician from Travancore, 'who could make one paralysed, or truly insane, or possessed of a devil,' should be sent for; wicked stories were told to the boy, in order to break down the gates of his will from another side. His sister and a little niece whom he dearly loved were brought to try to win him back. They fell at his feet, and clung to him, and wept. Orthodox Hindus, educated Hindus, and even a nominal Christian were brought to try to subvert his faith. They argued with him in vain. At last the father professed to agree to his being a Christian, reading his Bible, praying, even attending Church, if only he would consent to wear the Vishnu mark, the trident on his forehead, and the Brahman thread upon his shoulders. But God gave it to him to detect the snare in that delusive proposal, and braced him utterly to scorn it. After four months of confinement and mental strain, the boy was so reduced that it was thought he could not live long. It was very hot weather, and the jailers themselves found it irksome to keep guard in the little inner room; so, thinking he was too weak to escape, they allowed him to sleep unfettered on the verandah. One early morning, in the dark before the dawn, he felt as if an angel awakened him out of his sleep. He rose up, knelt down, and prayed for strength to walk. He was surrounded by people, but they did not wake. He dropped silently down into the street; strength came; the morning star, he said, was shining over his path. He ran through the streets, across the plain eleven miles to the Mission house, and was safe.

OJ 225

## Ragland — spiritual pioneer

Have we ever caught ourselves, as we looked at some old print, wondering if people so quaint felt exactly as we do? The woodcut in Perowne's Memoir [of Ragland] with its respectable Mission House, and top-hatted gentlemen, exceedingly prim ladies, and stiff clerics walking soberly in the background, feels milleniums remote from us and our ways. Did these decorously buttoned-up hearts beat hot as ours do? Were those so immaculate people really and truly up against life, with the tumble and toss of it, the laughter of it and the tears, its thousand secret shynesses, the tyrannies of temperament, and ignorings of the same?

See Ragland then and, to take him at his lowest ebb, see him in the soaking heat with a sermon in view. Now he bends over his paper, pen in hand, writes nothing; now sits back in his chair in a kind of despair, mopping his forehead, which drips, being, as the nice would put it, bedewed, and his hand, also plentifully 'bedewed', drips too and sticks to the paper. At last he begins again, but writes, in his deep desire, a prayer instead:

'Oh, help me to complete the preparation of my sermon: let it be suitable, wisely arranged; let it forcibly set before my people the important truths connected with my subject. Oh, let it not be as it were an essay, the performance of a task, the filling up of the half-hour.'

. . . . . .

[An extract from a sermon preached at Cambridge by Ragland in 1853 shortly before he sailed for India again — at his own expense and in ill health.]:

'If it had not been for a long chain of persecution and of shame and of humiliations and of labours and of self-denials and of prayers with strong crying and tears, we should not have the Gospel; and we cannot expect in any other way than by adding one link to that chain to have the glory of handing it down to

15

others. *If we refuse to be corn of wheat falling into the ground and dying; if we will neither sacrifice prospects, nor risk character and property and health; nor, when called, relinquish home and break family ties, for Christ's sake and His Gospel; then even supposing that we do not thereby prove that we have not the root of the matter in us, that we have nothing at all to do with Christ, we shall abide alone.'*

So he returned to India to live five glorious years and die a glorious death. . . . God forbid that we should be too careful of our lives, or of what means so immeasurably more, the lives of our beloved.

. . . . . .

June 3rd, 1851, a breathless date, for no rain from the western hills had come as yet to cool the air, and the pitiless heat of six parched months makes the average Englishman feel akin to the yellow stubble of grass in the dry watercourses. All flesh is grass, and withered grass, in June before the rains.

On that date, in that heat, Ragland wrote the words we copied before: *'Of all plans of ensuring success, the most certain in Christ's own, becoming a corn of wheat, falling into the ground, and dying.'*

June 11th, 1901, on just such a day, those same words were repeated slowly by a man like-minded — Walker of Tinnevelly. No life of Ragland was to be had then, but this one sentence was like a winged seed, it had flown down the fifty years to us. More than any other human words, they influenced the man who quoted them now.

On that day, sultry to exhaustion, after a long, sticky railway journey and a hotter, stickier bullock-cart drive, we had walked from the nearest mission station to Ragland's grave. A bare, baked road, six hot missionaries trudging along in more or less silence, for there was no visitor to delude into the belief that nobody was particularly tired — it does not sound an inspiring

16

spectacle. Nor was it. Dust lay thick everywhere, the heat was visible, as it is in our hottest days; you can see it in tremulous waves flowing knee-deep along the levels, breast-high sometimes where spaces are vast. The sun, knowing he was near his setting, thrust at us in long, sharp, slanting stabs, and the wind we longed for lay low and said nothing.

In silence, then, we stood beside the place where the shell of Ragland lay, near by the house where he had died. Desolation reigned. Not a green thing breathed. But that word, quick as the day it was first written on paper long since turned to dust, was at work then, is at work to-day, imperishable as energy.

*Verily, verily, I say unto you, 'Except a corn of wheat fall into the ground and die, it abideth alone; but if it die, it bringeth forth much fruit.'*

RSP 27, 63, 104, 111

### Shadow and coolness

In Southern India the wind is often hot, and hot air rises like a
burning breath from the ground. That is what gave a line to
this song. Such a wind parches the spirit, drains it of vitality,
sends it to seek some cool place, caring only to find a shadow
from the heat. But be the wind scorching, or sharp and cold, it
can only cause the spices of His garden to flow out. And often,
have we not found it so? The Lord of the garden calls His
south wind; and all the flowers know it is blowing, and are
glad.

Shadow and coolness, Lord, art Thou to me;
Cloud of my soul, lead on, I follow Thee.
What though the hot winds blow,
Fierce heat beat up below,
Fountains of water flow —
　　Praise, praise to Thee.

Clearness and glory, Lord, art Thou to me;
Light of my soul, lead on, I follow Thee.
All through the moonless night,
Making its darkness bright,
Thou art my heavenly Light —
　　Praise, praise to Thee.

Shadow and Shine art Thou, dear Lord, to me;
Pillar of Cloud and Fire, I follow Thee.
What though the way be long,
In Thee my heart is strong,
Thou art my joy, my song —
　　Praise, praise to Thee.

RB 82

18

## Adoration and worship

I believe that if we are to be and to do for others what God means us to be and to do, we must not let Adoration and Worship slip into the second place, 'For it is the central service asked by God of human souls; and its neglect is responsible for much lack of spiritual depth and power.' Perhaps we may find here the reason why we so often run dry. We do not give time enough to what makes for depth, and so we are shallow; a wind, quite a little wind, can ruffle our surface; a little hot sun, and all the moisture in us evaporates. It should not be so.

This has been our God's word to me afresh this morning and so I pass it on. Is it not worth-while earnestly to set ourselves towards this? Today, if we will hear His voice, today, this morning, if we will draw near to Him, He will draw near to us. In the hush of that nearness we shall not seek anything for ourselves, not even help, or light, or comfort; we shall forget ourselves, 'lost in wonder, love and praise.'

'Let us draw near hither unto God.' 'Let us follow on to know the Lord: we shall find Him ready as the morning.' The morning never disappoints us by not coming, neither does our loving God.

EW 55

19

Cause me to hear, for it is life to me;
I perish when I am away from Thee,
Love of my love,
Tell me, where walkest Thou?
I would be with Thee now.

Let me be Thy companion, even I,
For whom Thou once didst in a garden lie;
Love of my love,
Than all my dear more dear,
Tell me, may I draw near?

I may, I may. Thou callest me to come;
O Dweller in the gardens, this is home.
Love of my love,
Dear Lord, what would I more
But listen, serve, adore?

GC 176

## Windows

DANIEL 6.10. *He went into his house; and his windows being open in his chamber toward Jerusalem, he kneeled upon his knees . . . and prayed.*

Daniel did not have to open his windows when he wanted to commune with his Lord. Apparently they were open, as our Indian windows are, all the time. Is it not a perfect picture of how we are meant to live? We do not have to spend even one minute in opening our windows, if our custom is to keep them open. To be earthly-minded, moved by self-love, self-pity, self-will — that trend of feeling which leads to self-occupation — is to close the shutters.

Are my windows open toward Jerusalem? Is my whole being, with all its various 'windows', always open? Sometimes winds blow from one side or another and a window is blown shut. If that happens, do I know it at once?

Lord Jesus, let me know it at once. Do not let me go on with any windows shut or half-open. Lord, help me to keep my windows open continually toward Jerusalem.

EW 92

## Refreshment

Sometimes when we are tired we spend an hour with the poets' thought-music; word music holds a charm like the music of moving waters, to soothe and heal. Sometimes rest comes otherwise. The mystery of mighty spaces, the splendour of great forces, or the magic of colour, the marvel of the loveliness about us seems to open suddenly as if another finer sense than sight perceived it, and one's very being thrills with an incommunicable joy. Sometimes a different thing happens.

One can hardly tell what. Only one knows that, through and through, one is strong and glad and well again. One has seen part of the Ways of God.

OJ 16

## A pure work

Don't be surprised if there is attack on your work, on *you* who are called to do it, on your innermost nature — the hidden man of the heart. It must be so. The great thing is not to be surprised, not to count it strange — for that plays into the hand of the enemy.

Is it possible that anyone should set himself to exalt our beloved Lord and *not* become instantly a target for many arrows? The very fact that your work depends utterly on Him and can't be done for a moment without Him calls for a very close walk and a constant communion of spirit. This alone is enough to account for anything the enemy can do.

But there are limits set. Greater is He. I have just read that glorious word in Romans 5, 'They that receive the abundance of grace . . . reign in life, through the One, even Jesus Christ.' And this was written to slaves in Nero's wicked palace. What daring of faith the Spirit gave to Paul.

It *costs* to have a pure work. Not for nothing is our God called a Consuming Fire.

CD 31

## No third choice

In all the deeper missionary books there is sure to be some allusion to the power and deadliness of satanic attack upon the spirit of the missionary; but there is seldom detail given upon which one who wants to understand can lay hold. It sounds terrible but vague.

And yet the attack follows certain lines, such as these; during the dumb years of language study before the new roots have had time to grow, there may be discouragement; if the life that has been left was full to overflowing, almost certainly there will be the penetrating, hissing whisper, 'How much more you might have done for God at home!' After the language is learned and one is perhaps alone in idolatrous city or Muslim town, a black sea can sweep up, wave upon wave. 'Hell's foundations quiver,' says the hymn. It is one's own foundations that quiver under the impact of those tremendous floods. Or fierce temptation assail, and fiery darts rain on the naked soul.

Or there may be something different. A man's lot is cast where there is a mass of nominal Christianity. At first he feels it keenly and speaks sincerely. But gradually the sharp edges of feeling wear smooth. He slides into slack content. 'From slack contentment keep me free,' is a vital prayer.

To another is offered delicious spiritual flattery, and the soul has drunk deep of that enchantment or ever it is aware that it has drunk at all. But others know, for in speech and in writing he who has drunk of that cup mixes sugar with his salt.

Or the dark forces may work with inoffensive simplicity: a fog of depression descends, 'the climate is so trying', or pricks of irritation assail, 'we are so sensitive'; or there may be that discontent which the ancients called *accidie*; 'When this besieges the unhappy mind, it begets aversion from the place, boredom with one's cell, and scorn and contempt for one's brethren, whether they be dwelling with one or some way off, as careless and unspiritually-minded persons.' *(The Desert Fathers)* Or there may be just plain dryness, and somehow the missionary had never expected to feel dry.

'What is it?' he asks, astonished at the vehemence of these invasions. But the enemy never answers, 'It is I,' nor does the soul always say, 'Is it I?' It often lays the blame of weakness and defeat on something else, or on someone else, or on that convenient scapegoat, 'my circumstances.'

But there is deliverance for him who is set upon victory: *As for me, my feet were almost gone; my steps had well-nigh slipped. When I said, My foot slippeth; Thy mercy, O Lord, held me up.* There is never a fear that has not a corresponding 'Fear not'.

Every keen missionary values above rubies prayer that fortifies him along these lines. It is possible to lose ground because of some private refusal to the will of God at the point where it crossed our natural will, and if this happens, the Lord cannot fulfil His purpose through us. The purging of the inner man, if the sword is to be tempered for delicate and powerful use, can be a more searching experience than anything the missionary expected when first he sailed for his new home. And he must either welcome this purging and go through with it, or shrink back from it and fail. There is no third choice. It is a solemn thought.

W 50

## The price

There is a price to be paid. Sooner or later our Lord's words, as recorded in Luke 14.26, have to be wrought out in life. 'Discipleship involves the subordination of human relationships to the claims of the Lord Himself' (Reginald T. Naish). There is a sword that pierces even to the dividing asunder of soul and spirit, and of the joints and marrow. This is that. It cannot be evaded. Evasion never leads to blessing. 'Choose,' said a voice in the ear of one whom this sword was piercing, 'Choose if your loved ones are to know all I can be to them, or if they are to lose the best because they have you instead.' When the urgent temptation came to turn that sword from another, or at least to blunt its edge, the word was the same, 'Do so, and grievous loss will follow. There will not be any gain.'

TMS 161

## Loneliness

On this day many years ago I went away alone to a cave in a mountain called Arima, in Japan. I felt many feelings of fear about the future. That was why I went there. I wanted to be alone with God.

The devil kept on whispering, 'It's all right now, but what about afterwards? You are going to be very lonely.' And he painted pictures of loneliness. I can see them still. Then I turned to my God in a kind of desperation and said, 'Lord, what can I do? How can I go on to the end?' And he said, 'None of them that trust in Me shall be desolate' (Psalm 34.22).

That word has been with me ever since, and I give it to you now. It has been fulfilled to me. It will be fulfilled to you. Only live for Him who redeemed you and trust Him to take care of you, *and He will.*

That day the words 'not only but also' were given to me too. There is not only joy but also sorrow in every life, but in the end — O in the end we shall see His face and we shall serve Him together.

CD 17

## Training for service

The best training is to learn to accept everything as it comes, as from Him whom our soul loves. The tests are always unexpected things, not great things that can be written up, but the common little rubs of life, silly little nothings, things you are ashamed of minding one scrap. Yet they can knock a strong man over and lay him very low.

CD 2

## The gold that is Christ

My flesh and my heart faileth — let them fail. For God is the strength of my heart and my portion for ever. Has anyone ever been able to tell what our glorious Lord can be to man, woman, or little child whom He is training to wait upon Him only?

No one has ever been able to tell it. I search for words like jewels, or stars, or flowers, but I cannot find them. I wish I could, for this book may fall into the hands of someone who has been hindered from caring to know Him by the dull and formal trapping which our dull and formal thoughts have laid upon Him — strange disguise for such a radiance. How can I commend my Master? I have not seen Him yet, but I have caught glimpses. Human soul meets human soul, exploring feelers move out cautiously, albeit unconsciously, perhaps to draw back uncertain; it is better that there should be a little film of distance held between. But sometimes it is not like that. The warning instinct is not there. Instead there is a lovely freedom. Each is at home in the other's rooms. There is a joy in that sense of sureness, in understanding and in being understood. There is joy in the recognition of that which makes it safe to trust to the utmost of the utmost. What makes it so? It is the golden quality of love perfected in strength. That gold is Christ. Or some sharp test takes that friend unawares. You see the life reel under shattering blows; perhaps you see it broken. And you look almost in fear. Thus suddenly discovered, what will appear? And no base metal shows, not even the lesser silver, but only veins and veins of gold. That gold is Christ.

GC 62

26

## A question

On a lower slope of the hillside that lies under this kindling sky, a girl sat alone with earth and sky. Why was she not with her companions at the Pillar Rocks? She did not know. She could give them no reason why she could not join them; she only knew that though she had much wished to see that magnificence set in its deep ravine, she could not go with them. John Wesley's words when he turned from looking at a lovely view were haunting, 'I remembered there was an eternity,' but they did not seem reason enough. She had asked to be told why this constraint was upon her, but nothing had come; so she had settled to language study, and in grammar and dictionary forgot the Pillar Rocks.

She was sitting under a wide-spreading tree and all about her were the little sounds of bird and insect. A thousand tiny bells rang tiny chimes among the grass, and there were rustlings, and the soft murmurings of wind among leaves; but she heard without hearing. Tamil was so absorbing; till through the multitudinous voices another Voice began to speak. *'The voice of thy brother's blood,'* it said, *'crieth unto Me from the ground.'*

It was a strange moment, strange in its complete surprise. After that, for a while, time ceased for the girl under the tree. Morning passed into noon, afternoon faded slowly, then lit in the shining sky of evening, and the picnic party came home; but all that is a blur. The vivid, unforgettable thing is what happened through those hours that were not measured hours.

First and chiefly there was an enfolding sense of a Presence, a Listener. He was listening to the voice of our brother's blood crying unto Him from the ground. That voice was crying to Him everywhere. And He looked for some to listen with Him. Wilt thou listen with Me? He said; canst thou not watch with Me one hour? for a life of hours — with Me?

But to write is to fumble among things of the spirit, and yet some words were clear. 'Many follow Jesus unto the breaking of bread, but few unto the drinking of the cup of the passion'; art thou willing to drink of that cup, and to drink it unto the end? Art thou willing to refuse all that would interrupt the drinking of that cup? Art thou willing to turn from all that would dull thine ear to the voice of thy brother's blood that crieth unto Me from the ground?

That day under the tree on the hillside in South India coloured the years that were to follow and gave depth to them all. It lay behind that other hour when the voice of the blood was the cry of little children; it led to the prayer for words to tell of that cry; the prayer that was answered thus:

Thou shalt have words
But at this cost, that thou must first be burnt.
Burnt by red embers from a secret fire,
Scorched by fierce heats and withering winds that sweep
Through all thy being, carrying thee afar
From old delights . . .
Not otherwise, and by no lighter touch,
Are fire-words wrought.

Once or twice in a generation someone writes a revealing book, or even only a chapter in a book. We read, and the decorous green turf that covers the meadow of life is ripped off, and the ground opens at our feet. And as we read, we see . . .

Then what did we do? Did the feeling that welled up within us slowly drain away till we look back on that hour of revelation with a kind of wonder, a mild wonder that we ever cared so much? Emotion that does nothing ends in a morass.

But what could we do? We should have been like a straw before a flood had we tried to stem the torrent of iniquity of which we had at last become aware. We say this to ourselves

28

and to others, and others say it to us. But need the soul redeemed at Calvary, and energized by the Eternal Spirit, ever be like a straw before a flood?

W 236

# 1901 — 1930

The work known as the Dohnavur Fellowship
began in 1901 and most of these readings
relate to life at Dohnavur.

## No Scar?

Hast thou no scar?
No hidden scar on foot, or side, or hand?
I hear thee sung as mighty in the land,
I hear them hail thy bright ascendant star,
Hast thou no scar?

Hast thou no wound?
Yet I was wounded by the archers, spent,
Leaned Me against a tree to die; and rent
By ravening beasts that compassed Me, I swooned:
Hast *thou* no wound?

No wound? no scar?
Yet, as the Master shall the servant be,
And piercèd are the feet that follow Me;
But thine are whole: can he have followed far
Who has nor wound nor scar?

TJ 85

32

## The coming of Pearleyes

We should have been as others who see without seeing, and never dream of what is being done out of sight, if it had not been for what was caused to happen on March 6th, 1901. . . .

Pearleyes, a child of seven, whose father, a thoughtful and scholarly Hindu landowner, had recently died, was allowed by her mother to pay a visit to women of whose occupation that mother knew little. They were servants of the gods, women belonging to a temple sacred to Perumal, one of the incarnations of Vishnu, in a village called Great Lake. This meant that each had been 'married to the god', and that meant deified sin.* In this child they saw one who could be trained to live that life, and they let her see things likely to accustom her to iniquity, and thus, according to the Tamil saying that what is not bent at five will be unbendable at fifty, tried to bend the mind of this child to their purposes.

But Pearleyes recoiled from it all. Perhaps a natural perversity of character had something to do with it; but far more surely a certain purity of spirit and instinctive horror of every false way worked within her, and she fled from the evil house. Her home was in Tuticorin, a town on the south-east coast, two days' journey by cart from Great Lake. How could so young a child go so far alone? It would take much more than two days to walk there. She trudged off bravely. Friendly carters gave her a lift occasionally, and at last that valiant little thing found her mother's house in the big and wicked town, one of the Sodoms of this province, and she flung herself into her mother's arms, sure of safe haven there.

---

* Legislation in the Madras Legislative Assembly in 1947 prohibited the dedication of little girls to Hindu temples in the Madras State. An act passed by the Central Government in Delhi in 1954 made it illegal in the whole of India.

But the temple-women had followed. They threatened the mother with the wrath of the gods. Her husband had been a devout Hindu. He had been famous as a reader and expounder of the religious poetry of his nation. The fear of the gods was upon the mother. She tore her little child's arms from her neck and pushed her back to those women, and they carried her off in triumph.

This decided them to marry her to [the god] Perumal as soon as possible, and Pearleyes overheard their conversation, and thought that the idiom 'tied to the god' meant that she would be tied with ropes to the figure of the idol she had seen in the far recesses of the temple, and, terrified, she made up her mind to risk any punishment and tried to escape again.

But she was jealously watched — such children are of value to their possessors; there were eyes everywhere.

One day — it was a day of terror for that helpless child — she crossed the stone-paved floor of the temple court and, going into the dark inner cell where the idol was set, threw herself down and prayed to Perumal to let her die.

At that time we were in Dohnavur, on the western side of the district, and were about to return to Great Lake, our old centre in the east where previously we had been itinerating. We left Dohnavur on March 4th, travelling, as was usual then, by night, to escape slow travel through the heat. We arrived at our old house on the 6th. That evening something happened in the temple-house in the village of Great Lake. What happened? . . .

And behold an angel of the Lord, saying, Arise up quickly. Pearleyes saw no angel, heard no voice, but someone must have touched her and said, Follow me. For she followed, and no one saw her. Down the village street she walked, past the temple walls, and no one stopped her. Across the stream, through a little grove of palms and on to the village beyond she ran, and then stood waiting. There a kindly woman found her,

34

like a lost lamb looking for its fold, and she took her home for the night. Servant of Jesus thought at first of taking the little one back to her home, but mercifully it was late (another touch of the hand of God) and so instead she took her straight to her own little house, which satisfied Pearleyes perfectly.

. . . . . .

Next morning again the woman's first thought was to take her to her own people. But the child was so insistent that she wanted the child-catching Ammal, that Servant of Jesus, thinking I was the Ammal she meant (for this is one of my various names) brought her to me, and oh, I am glad she did!

I was sitting reading in the verandah when I saw them come. The woman was looking surprised. She did not know about the Angel, I expect, and she could not understand it at all. The little child was chattering away, lifting up a bright little face as she talked. When she saw me she ran straight up to me, and climbed on my knee without the least fear, and told me all about herself at once. . . .

'My name is Pearleyes,' the child began, 'and I want to stay here always. I have come to stay.'

. . . . . .

The child told us things that darkened the sunlight. It was impossible to forget those things. Wherever we went after that day we were constrained to gather facts about what appeared a great secret traffic in the souls and bodies of young children, and we searched for some way to save them and could find no way. The helpless little things seemed to slip between our fingers as we stretched out our hands to grasp them, or it was as though a great wave swept up and carried them out to sea. In a kind of desperation, we sought for a way. But we found that we must know more before we could hope to find it. To graze upon the tips (of herbage) is the Tamil synonym for superficial knowledge. If we were to do anything for these children it was vain to graze on the tips of facts; it took years to do more than that. . . .

We discovered nothing by asking questions. To ask was to close every door. To be foreign in dress, food or ways would have been to lock those doors, the only doors to knowledge. We learned by quietly sharing as much as we could in the life of the people, by listening, not by questioning. Ponnamal, one of the three Indian sisters of those early days, used to travel with me, and together we stayed in some wayside shelter, often only a roof on pillars, or with a convert girl who had married and lived in a temple town. Once we camped in a byre in a city slum, and Ponnamal, who had never slept on a dirty floor, comforted herself by remembering Bethlehem. Wherever a mat could be spread on the ground, there we stayed for as long as we could stand the noise and glare and heat and smells. . . .

We had found that the children in peril belonged to five groups. . . . Children are dedicated to the temple because of a vow, or in obedience to a family custom, or in order to escape from some social entanglement caused, for example, by an out-of-caste alliance. Often a poor widow or a deserted wife of good family, faced with the impossibility of marrying her child suitably, marries her to the god. Sometimes lack of money to perform the death ceremonies required by the caste tempts a mother to part with her child for her husband's sake. And whenever a caste child is without protectors, there is danger. In certain parts of India caste is not considered, but in the South it is.

Everywhere there are men and women on the watch for these children. The sale of a child is illegal; but money is not passed in public, and the necessary proof cannot be obtained. The woman who buys the child calls it her own daughter, and can easily get witnesses to prove the relationship. . . .

And now a great urgency was upon us. We thirsted for the strong succour of prayer for the children. We were still

36

itinerating, camping in different parts of the district, seldom for long in one place, learning all we could wherever we went, becoming daily more burdened.

We were camping in Dohnavur, then a bare, sunburnt spot out on the plains under the mountains to the west, a huddle of huts and small houses round a fairly big, whitewashed church with, beyond low mud walls, an old ramshackle bungalow built of mud bricks and visibly falling to pieces, when two friends came to stay with us. They asked me to tell what I could of things just as they were. There was no time to sit down and write a book — there never has been time for anything so leisured — but they suggested putting together some home letters already written, and so *Things as They Are* began with the ordinary missionary day of the time before the first little temple-child came. But it soon reached the place where words seemed of no use at all.

'What thou seest, write.' But how? How write anguish? . . . On a day when any words that I could find seemed wholly inadequate, on a page torn from an old exercise-book something was written down, with no thought of print:

> Thou shalt have words,
> But at this cost, that thou must first be burned. . . .

And so at last words came.

GC 20—30; TTA

## Fire-Words

'O God, my words are cold:
The frosted frond of fern or feathery palm
Wrought on the whitened pane —
They are as near to fire as these my words;
Oh that they were as flames!' Thus did I cry,
And thus God answered me: 'Thou shalt have words,
But at this cost, that thou must first be burnt,
Burnt by red embers from a secret fire,
Scorched by fierce heats and withering winds that sweep
Through all thy being, carrying thee afar
From old delights. Doth not the ardent fire
Consume the mountain's heart before the flow
Of fervent lava? Wouldst thou easefully,
As from cool, pleasant fountains, flow in fire?
Say, can thy heart endure or can thy hands be strong
In the day that I shall deal with thee?

'For first the iron must enter thine own soul,
And wound and brand it, scarring awful lines
Indelibly upon it, and a hand
Resistless in a tender terribleness
Must thoroughly purge it, fashioning its pain
To power that leaps in fire.
Not otherwise, and by no lighter touch,
Are fire-words wrought.'

WT 254

38

## *Dohnavur*

Near the little jungle village of Dohnavur, in the old wreck of a compound (haunted by flocks of noisy goats) that surrounded the decrepit, three-roomed bungalow, there were four cottages . . . There was no thought then of staying in Dohnavur for more than a year, but the children had begun to come, and children cannot be carted about. So the Walkers made the place their headquarters, and we continued, to our great comfort, to live with them there . . .

After the work for the children developed we understood why this special place had been chosen for our home. It is several miles from the road, and in those days it was even more inaccessible than it is now, so it was not only safer for the children than a town would have been, it was good for us too; for we were free to serve without too many interruptions. It was healthy (that is, for the tropics), there was no malaria. It was beautiful, too, because of the mountains to the west of the village. These mountains were a wonderful help. They were so unchangeably strong and tranquil and serene that just to look at them strengthened us. Often, caught and tangled in the throng of things, we used to stop and let their calmness enter into us, and we prayed that we might serve with 'a quiet mind'. It was not a question of choice with us now. If we were to go on at all, we must have a quiet mind. We had already seen more than one missionary break down, not because of the climate or the work, but because of a wearied, fretted spirit too rushed to dwell in peace. So this prayer was not for a spiritual luxury, but for sheer necessity, and as the children grew up we taught it to them, and tried to help them also to serve Him with a quiet mind, so that in all our rooms there should be peace.

GC 39

If you approach Dohnavur from the South, you find yourself in a village street, and, turning in at the gate that opens off the street, you pass through a moon-arch with *Salvation* on the outer side, and *Praise* on the inner, set clear upon it in Tamil script. And then you are in the protective courtyard of the children's world.

This has for its western wall the old bungalow, built perhaps a hundred and fifty years ago, now very decrepit. The walls of some of its rooms are striped in rainy weather with long, untidy, reddish patches, and the whole house clamours for large repairs, re-roofing and the like. But, in spite of that, it sets us all an example of good-tempered fortitude, for it stays up. Two gates open into the compound which is home to so many happy children.

And now, if you are a casual person, you will see only trees, little houses, children big and small, and a central building, Indian in feeling, fitting into its place as chief House of all our houses. Most of our buildings have the deep-eaved Travancore roofs, and some have the curly corners that the Chinese carpenters brought to the west coast of India, and all, even the moon-arches, which are pure China, find themselves at home with one another: and, like our composite family, drawn from a score of different races, communities, and castes, are very comfortable together.

## The children

As all who know us know, the children are the core of the work. And our greatest need always is for the chosen and prepared worker to train these boys and girls for our Lord's service. It takes a long time to prepare such a worker. It takes years.

For our dear children are not easy to train. The Indian child hates the difficult and avoids it if possible. Slackness meets us everywhere. And yet there is a curious opposite quality latent in the Indian nature. Could you clench your hand and hold it so, till your finger-nails grew through the back of your hand? The Indian can. So in dealing with Indian character one must remember these opposites, a will which shirks the hard, and a will which can set itself, perhaps in some futile or harmful direction, and can keep set.

But there is a charm about the Indian child, something like the sparkle on water, a charm that cannot be captured in words. Above all there is love. How often we are hushed in heart as we come on some token of a love which knows nothing of boundaries; for when India loves, she loves with her whole mind and strength. It is a wonderful thing to be allowed to offer all that we have, to lead a people who can love like that, to the One who alone is worthy to receive such treasure.

What touches those who visit us, and have hearts to care, is the sight of the children, merry, welcoming children, who might have been like little Goddess of Holy Town (she is called after a god) who came one day to see us, chaperoned by an observant old lady. We have known her since she was a baby, and she is now devoted to temple service. Can you see a slim, graceful girl in a soft silk sari, with a long plait down her back, and a face like a flower? But there is a look in that face which no one has ever seen in the face of a flower — an aloof look. When she smiled that day her smile was aloof, almost enigmatic. That smile was sadder than tears.

There were no tears when we pleaded with her to forsake her terrible life, as she is old enough now to choose, and could come to us if she wished, and if she dared to face the storm that would follow. But she said, 'Holy Town is preparing for a festival, I am engaged to dance before the idol through the whole night.' Poor flower; she never had a chance; she was bent in the wrong way from her babyhood. And our Lotus Buds might have been like that.

TMS 32

41

## Thy Golden Cord

Our Sovereign Leader and belovèd Lord,
Make strong the threads of this Thy golden cord,
Make fast the knot that binds us one in Thee
In loyalty.

Let holy fealty be our bond sincere,
Let us be each to other crystal-clear,
Clear as the jasper in Thy City wall,
So keep us all.

O keep us facing toward Jerusalem;
Steep are the hills, let us not turn from them.
Let us go forward as one company,
Rejoicingly.

W

### The Butterfly — An Action Song

Our mother was a butterfly,
   We are her little eggs,
Inside us caterpillars lie,
   Young things with many legs.

I am a little caterpillar,
   Very soft and fat,
I'll change into a chrysalis,
   What do you think of that?

I am a little chrysalis,
   And very still I lie;
For folded up inside me
   Is a little butterfly.

I am the little butterfly,
   I want to fly about;
I'm so tired of being here —
   Oh, now I'm out! I'm out!

O kind wind, come and fan my wings,
   O sunshine, make them dry,
O flower, I come to you! Away,
   Away, away I fly.

ACD 239

## A *missionary journey*

After a while we were allowed to take Star with us when we were out in camp. The freshness of dew is on those memories, though anything less like dew than the blistering heat, when there are no large trees and the tents have to be pitched under palmyra palms on blazing sand, can hardly be imagined. When it was cool it was also wet, so that camp generally meant the dry season and heat. But nothing mattered. We were strong with the joy of morning.

And we had need to be, for our journeys were not luxurious. They were wholly delightful, however, especially for Star. What could have been more enjoyable than the start, in a long comical procession of bullock bandies, each one packed inside with people, and festooned outside with all manner of things? Pots and pans and buckets, a kettle or two, bundles of firewood, bulgy sacks of oddments that had not gone in the baggage-cart, were roped to the sides of the curved mat roof and made a cheerful clatter. Each bandy had a heap of straw piled on the top of the roof or slung in a net underneath, where also was hung an earthen cruse of water and probably a basketful of fowls. Their cackle mixed with the general racket, the jingle of the bullock bells, and the shouts of the drivers made a most exciting noise. Just as we were about to start a bandy-driver would melt into the dusk — he had not yet had his curry and rice, a fellow-carter would kindly explain; or we would discover that one of the bandies had forgotten its lantern, and the whole procession would be held up while that lantern was retrieved and tied to the bandy or swung to the pole just out of reach of the bullocks' tails. It was hot inside the bandies and unbelievably stuffy, for the bare and glistening brown back of the driver filled up most of the open end in front, and, in our cart at least, there were always three, which meant that if one of us wanted to turn all must turn; but it was pure bliss.

Camp had its merry times, for Star had a scandalous habit of playing pranks on the somewhat sober-minded older women of the band. One day we returned from work to be met outside my tent by growls, snarls, barks, scuffling. 'Dogs! *Chee!*' I can see their good brown faces wrinkled up in amazement as, with uplifted hands, they gasped, 'But no dogs be!' till a paroxysm of yelps suddenly tailed off into laughter and dishevelled Star wriggled out from under the low camp cot in the corner.

Star was all eagerness over other things too. I can see the bullock-cart drawn up near the door of the tent; the bulls loosely tethered, munching straw steadily; a knot of small girls and their attendant babies round the yoke-and-pole end; and perched on the pole, Star, 'preaching'.

Her small hearers were listening spellbound. I wondered what she was saying, something interesting, certainly. She had a way of her own of saying things. Once she happened to be alone on the verandah at night, with a lamp set behind her, so that it cast a small circle of light round her as she sat on the floor. When I asked her how long she had been alone she answered gravely: 'I have not been alone. There are five here: God the Father, God the Son, and God the Holy Spirit, the devil and me. But the devil', she added with great calmness, 'is outside there,' pointing to the darkness beyond the circle of lamplight.

PU 79

## Star

Arulai Tara [Star] was one whom the burdens of leadership would not have broken. From her very early days we had trained her with this thought in view. That is why the steel that was her soul was so often hammered out, plunged into the water, purified by fire. Nothing was ever made easy for her. She was too precious to spoil by the easy. In her was straightness, love, humility, and a devotion that never said 'Enough'. There was also that quality which bears up under trial; she did not give way when the sharp wind blew.

TMS 175

## The crimson garment

I think my story must have made it plain that when man or woman, boy or girl, dares to break through the opposing powers of death and hell and openly follow the Crucified, something inevitably and often immediately happens, as though to fling that life on the ground, and stamp it underfoot. It is usually illness, or accident, something that looks like the hand of the avenging god. Then it is that the writing on the soul, invisible till now, appears, made legible, as it were, by the hot iron of this burning experience. One who understands that writing can read strange things there. 'All night long the lizards cheeped' says much to one who knows the thought of the East.

But after the first assault has been repulsed there may be another, often many others, and so it was with Star. Twenty days after the day when for the first time she ate of the Bread and drank of the Wine, she was tossing in high fever, and the puzzled apothecary from the next village was suggesting a mixture of remedies, some Indian, some foreign; and we were beset behind and before by the clamours of relatives, who were sure beyond a doubt that this second illness was the signal sign of the wrath of the offended god.

It was typhoid fever; pneumonia followed; she all but died. First Supu, now Star. Was it strange that her family saw in such smashing blows an inescapable retribution, and trembled, asking 'What next?'

A friend came most lovingly then to help us nurse her, and we wrestled for her life. The word expresses that struggle. It was like fighting a tangible foe. It was never a wrestle with a reluctant Father (God forbid), but with His enemy and ours. I write this clearly because of the strange phrase 'wrestling with God' which is often used about such prayer. There is a wrestle, but it is with those all but palpable powers that seek to intervene between us and our God. And in the end we are given the desire of our hearts.

I know that sometimes we do not see how the thing granted is at all what we desire. And yet it is. For, after all, what the deepest in us wanted was not our own natural will, but the will of our Father. So what is given *is* our hearts' desire. He hath not withholden the request of our lips. *But God always answers us in the deeps, never in the shallows of our soul;* in hours of confusion, to remember this can help.

We had no doctor to pilot us through that illness, but a medically-minded missionary came several times and did all that he could for us. 'Is it well with the child? It is well,' he wrote across her chart when things were at their worst, and he said pitifully about me: 'She will have to give her up.' There were hours, day and night, when the only thing to be done was to hold on and refuse to let the frail little thread of her life slip through our fingers. There was one night — Star lay unconscious all that night — when in a shrine near the house the noise of tom-tom and cymbal sounded rampant in exultation over what seemed like another triumph for the gods. The weird shrieks of excited worshippers cut through the dark air between us and the shrine in a sort of fury, and there came a rush of voices that seemed to fill the room. But the peace of God was round about us. His peace was nearer than the noise, and so it continued to be all the time. When the child's parents came and stood by her cot waiting to break into the death-wail, when their accusing eyes were upon us and we could explain nothing, words cannot tell what it was to be folded in the peace of God.

47

Star came back from the gates of death a fragile shadow of herself. Her long hair had been cut off, of course, and her curly head made her look like a boy. She was so light that I could pick her up in my arms, and often did, carrying her over the rough places when we went out in the evenings, and wishing in my heart that I could carry her so over all the rough roads of life — weak wish, and futile. Ours is a God who delivers, not from the hour of trial, but out of it, out of its power; and in the bearing up under it, not in the sliding out from beneath it, there is strength and victory. 'Say, O Lover,' asked the Beloved, 'if I double thy trials, wilt thou still be patient?' 'Yea,' answered the Lover, 'so that Thou double also my love.' 'The Beloved clothed Himself in the garments of His Lover, that he might be His companion in glory for ever. So the Lover desired to wear crimson garments daily, that his dress might be like that of his Beloved.'

PU 113

## Ride Forth Singing

*If thou hast a fearful thought, share it not with a weakling, whisper it to thy saddle-bow, and ride forth singing.*

*King Alfred the Great*

Have I fear that Thou dost know?
Fear of weakness, fear of failing
(Though Thy power is all prevailing);
Or a haunting fear of bringing
Care to others?
Share it not with a weakling,
*Whisper it to thy saddle-bow,*
*And ride forth singing.*

Many fears can murmur low,
Fear of ills the future holdeth
(Though indeed Thy grace upholdeth),
Dulling fear and fear sharp-stinging,
Fear that tortures;
Share it not with a weakling,
*Whisper it to thy saddle-bow,*
*And ride forth singing.*

EW 146

49

## The goldsmith

One day we took the children to see a goldsmith refine gold after the ancient manner of the East. He was sitting beside his little charcoal fire. (He shall sit as a refiner: the gold- or silversmith never leaves his crucible once it is on the fire.) In the red glow lay a common curved roof-tile; another tile covered it like a lid. This was the crucible. In it was the medicine made of salt, tamarind fruit and burnt brick-dust, and embedded in it was the gold. The medicine does its appointed work on the gold, 'then the fire eats it', and the goldsmith lifts the gold out with a pair of tongs, lets it cool, rubs it between his fingers, and if not satisfied puts it back again in fresh medicine. This time he blows the fire hotter than it was before, and each time he puts the gold into the crucible the heat of the fire is increased: 'It could not bear it so hot at first, but it can bear it now; what would have destroyed it then helps it now.' 'How do you know when the gold is purified?' we asked him, and he answered, 'When I can see my face in it [the liquid gold in the crucible] then it is pure.'

GC 69

## 'Just to love you'

Sometimes in Dohnavur we, who dearly love the little children about us (and the older ones too), have looked up from some engrossing work to see a child beside us, waiting quietly. And when, with a welcoming hand held out, to the Tamil 'I have come', we have asked 'For what?' thinking, perhaps, of something to be confessed, or wanted, the answer has come back, 'Just to love you.' So do we come, Lord Jesus; we have no service to offer now; we do not come to ask for anything, not even for guidance. We come just to love Thee.

RB 121

## Clouds

This evening the clouds lay low on the mountains, so that sometimes we could hardly see them, and sometimes the stars were nearly all covered. But always, just when it seemed as though the mountains were going to be quite lost in the mist, the higher peaks pushed out, and whereas the dimmer stars were veiled, the brighter ones shone through. Even supposing the clouds had wholly covered the face of the mountains, and not a star had shone through the piled-up masses, the mountains would still have stood steadfast, and the stars would not have ceased to shine.

I thought of this and found it very comforting, simple as it is. Our feelings do not affect God's facts. They may blow up like clouds and cover the eternal things that we do most truly believe. We may not see the shining of the promises, but still they shine; and the strength of the hills that is His also, is not for one moment less because of our human weakness.

Heaven is no dream. Feelings go and come like clouds, but the hills and the stars abide.

EW 44

51

## Acceptance

The saving salt in a household which is the centre of various activities is that, whatever the preoccupation of the hour may be, the duty of life goes on oblivious of feelings. Just then friends at home were sending us a number of old books to distribute among English-reading pastors and teachers, and when the postman staggered up to the house laden with a sack of book packets and poured them out in a heap on the dining-room floor, we had to unpack them and put them away. Somehow one went astray, and reappeared later on my table, a thin, small book in faded brown, Adolph Monod's *Farewell*, published in 1873. It was not attractive — in fact it looked distinctly stodgy. I opened it without enthusiasm. It was the hot hour when the mind moves sluggishly; mine drowsed till suddenly, startled, I came upon this.

And if among the trials that you are called to bear there is one that seems, I do not say heavier than the others, but more compromising to your ministry, and likely to ruin for ever all the hopes of your holy mission, if outward temptations be added to these coming from within, if all seems assailed, body, mind, spirit, if all seems lost without remedy, well, accept this trial, shall I say, or this assemblage of trials, in a peculiar feeling of submission, hope and gratitude, as a trial in which the Lord will cause you to find a new mission. Hail it as the beginning of a ministry of weakness and bitterness, which the Lord has reserved for the last because the best, and which He will cause to abound in more living fruit than your ministry of strength and joy in days gone by ever yielded.

The words pierced to the heart of things in a way no other words have done.

Would it be truly so? Would what had seemed only hurtful to our ministry turn to blessing and power and joy? Was this something to be accepted with hope and gratitude? And now He who guides even to the sending of books caused a friend to lend us one just then which gave us this:

The old nature dies as He died. That which we were by nature, peacemakers, centres of happiness, dies as the corn of wheat dies, or rather appears to die as it passes out of sight, in order that it may reappear in a glorious resurrection form. If by God's help we hold fast in humble submission and childlike trust to our Lord while the dying is being accomplished, then our prayers for others have a tremendous power in His name, and either here or hereafter we find that we, like our Lord, have lifted up those for whom we prayed by His own resurrection force. (Bishop Wilkinson)

It is the eternal in books that makes them our friends and teachers — the paragraphs, the verses, that grip memory and ring down the years like bells, or call like bugles, or sound like trumpets; words of vision that open to us undying things and fix our eyes on them. . . . We are not here to be overcome, but to rise unvanquished after every knock-out blow, and laugh the laugh of faith, not fear.

And so, as week followed week, the vicious whisper Why? lost its power, and peace flowed in and filled every crevice of our being, till at last a day came when awed and almost broken by so great a gladness that we could only worship and wonder, we saw what had been bitterness in the cup turned into sweetness, even into the very wine of joy. . . .

In this short chapter I have packed the fine gold of many years, but instead of the word 'submission' in the far-reaching thought of the French teacher I should write *acceptance,* for more and more, as life goes on, that word opens doors into rooms of infinite peace, and the heart that accepts asks nothing, for it is at rest, and the pilgrim of love does not need a map or chart: 'I know my road, it leadeth to His heart.'

GC 309

For the ills that might have been
But were neither heard nor seen,
For the fire that did not burn us,
Deeps that could not drown nor turn us,
For our daily blessings, Lord,
Be Thy name adored.

For the gentle joys that pass
Like the dew upon the grass,
New each morning, lighting duty
With a radiance and a beauty,
For our daily blessings, Lord,
Be Thy name adored.

For the storm that threatened loud
And then melted like a cloud,
Seeking to distress, confound us,
Met Thy great wings folded round us,
For our daily blessings, Lord,
Be Thy name adored.

GC 314

## The house of prayer

But under this happiness and peacefulness there is going on ceaselessly a hand-to-hand fight with malevolent powers. Many an hour is spent by one and another in what St. Paul calls wrestling. For the devil and his myrmidons are never off duty, souls lately plucked from their grasp are assailed and plots are formed for their undoing. There is need for us to be sensitive to the approach of the enemy. We should know, before the wolf cometh and teareth the sheep, that he is near and threatening. There is something the hireling can teach us here; he seeth the wolf coming.

> O Lord, make me aware
> Of peril in the air,
> Before the wolf can leap
> Upon the sheep.
>
> Give me the eye that sees
> When he is threatening these
> Who are so dear to Thee,
> So dear to me.

And so, because deadly things can be attempted even in our quiet compound after the chimes have played 'Abide with me', we do not find the long silence of our evening Communion too long. For the hour is full of silence, broken only by the voice of our Tamil pastor, and by versicles of adoration and worship, sung kneeling. The House is white then, and the whiteness of the Indian garments and the stillness, and the very gentle movement and the singing, have a ministry of their own, and often there is a sense of a Presence manifest and all but visible.

That Presence draws so near that loving little things like this can happen: one sultry evening a worshipper, almost too tired to kneel, thought of the first Supper — Now there was leaning on Jesus' bosom one of His disciples whom Jesus loved. 'Oh, that I might!' It was not a prayer, hardly a formed wish, only a little tired longing to lean; but One is with us who is closer than breathing, and there was a sudden sweetness and then, 'You may'.

And after the hymn that closes our Communion had been sung (it is always that perfect hymn, 'Jesus, Thou joy of loving hearts'), and the soft sound of bare feet walking softly had passed, that tired one, refreshed as a withered flower by heavenly dews, went out, to find a Hindu friend waiting near the door. This friend had often wondered whether our Lord Jesus spoke to us in words that we could understand. And just as a hidden fragrance finds its way out into the air, so does a private sweetness. So his question was answered then.

GC 299

## On prayer

We grew into a kind of prayer that is, for us at least, very helpful. We ask to be led by the Holy Spirit from point to point, each prayer leading on from the preceding prayer till the particular subject laid on our hearts has been dealt with, and we have the assurance that the Lord will complete all, as Kay translates Psalm 138.8.

This way of prayer is just the opposite to the kaleidoscope kind, which darts hither and thither all over the earth or over a number of scattered interests (often within the limits of a single long prayer) leaving the mind which has tried to follow perhaps dazzled, perhaps tired. It is a much simpler thing. Such prayer is often brief; it is often silent, or it may take the form of a song, and we are lifted up as with wings to our Lord's feet. It is possible only when all who are praying together do thoroughly understand one another, are, indeed, as one instrument under the control of the Spirit of God, who moves on each severally as He will, or unites all in silence or in song. Such prayer asks for something not easily defined. Darby's translation of Exodus 23.21, 'Be careful in His Presence,' comes to mind as a word that expresses its quietness and awe, and the jubilant psalms show its joy.

The habit of having a settled prayer day once a month was a great help. It led to something which we could not do without now — occasional extra days when we plan, so that the many whirling wheels of our busy world shall run down as much as possible, and we be set free to give ourselves to prayer. 'Do not be so busy with work for Christ that you have no strength left for praying,' said Hudson Taylor once. 'True prayer requires strength.' To secure even half a day's quiet in a large family like ours needs careful planning beforehand, but it is worth that. Again and again things have happened after such a day that nothing we could have done could have effected, for prayer is truly force. So when the constraint is upon us we yield to it, believing it to be of God. Sometimes to one or another privately this compulsion comes, and we have a quiet room set apart for this purpose; no one goes there except for quietness. When it comes to all, then, after we have had some time alone, we meet as on our usual prayer day, and this way of being together in prayer is a strand in our gold cord.

GC 77

## On asking God for something

One of the earliest lessons we learned together was that before asking for anything we should find out if it were according to the mind of the Lord. The kind of prayer that is a pouring out of the heart is different. This, that was definite petition, intercession, needed preparation of a special kind. It needed time — time to listen, to understand, to 'wait', as the word is so often in the Psalms. And this is the confidence that we have in Him that *if we ask anything according to His will He heareth us:* and if we know that He hear us whatsoever we ask, *we know that we have* the petitions that we desired of Him. The more we pondered over all that is said about prayer in the only book in the world that can speak with authority about it, the more we found to make us ask to be filled with the knowledge of His will before offering petitions for a desired good. When we were in doubt about His will (as we often were and are) and had not liberty to ask for a clear sign, there was the prayer of prayers ready framed for us: Thy will be done, whatever that will may be. But when we are meant to know our Lord's wishes, we must be shown what they are before we can lay our prayer alongside, and often our first prayer was for spiritual understanding and direction in prayer:

> That which I know not teach Thou me.
> Who, blessed Lord, teacheth like Thee?
> Lead my desires that they may be
>     According to Thy will.

> Kindle my thoughts that they may glow,
> And lift them up where they are low,
> And freshen them, that they may flow
>     According to Thy will.

We did not know Julian, the dear Anchoress of Norwich,

then; but later we knew her, and found this that we were
learning had been written down by her five hundred years
before: 'I am the Ground of Thy beseeching,' she wrote, as she
believed the words came to her from her Lord Himself. 'First it
is My will that thou have it; and after I make thee to will it;
and after, I make thee beseech it; and thou beseechest it. How
should it then be that thou shouldst not have thy beseeching?'

GC 48

## His thoughts said — his Father said

How very little, we have often found ourselves thinking as we took a visitor round nurseries, schoolrooms, playgrounds, hospital, or even out to the villages where much of our work directly and indirectly lies — how very little is ever seen of what really is. We pass a girl who looks up from her work and smiles, 'What a happy face!' says the guest. We pass a rampageous bunch of boys, 'I have never seen happier lads.' And yet all the time a relentless war is being waged against forces incalculable in subtlety and strength. We are continually looking at invisible battlefields. That girl who smiled so cheerily is going through a test of fortitude and constancy, which, could she know it, would send the visitor speechless to her knees. One of those merry boys lately fought, and by God's grace won, in a conflict of which none caught the slightest glimpse but those who had his deepest confidence. And it is so everywhere. Not one is overlooked by the enemy unless he slip out of the firing-line. When that happens there may be a great calm — but it is the calm of death.

Thank God, many are learning to use the very winds that seek to uproot them, as the pilot of the sailplane (taught by the birds) uses the winds and the currents of the air. But the soul sometimes tires, even as it rises. Effortless ease and spiritual uprising and the lifting of others do not run together, ever.

At one time some of the thoughts which were trying to disturb the peace of faithful workers were put into words thus:

*His thoughts said, When I would seek Him whom my soul loveth, confusions like flies buzz about me.*

His Father said, Press through these confusions as thou wouldest press through a swarm of gnats. Take no notice of them. Be not stayed by them. Be not occupied with them.

61

*His thoughts said, It is too much to hope that such a one as I am should truly please my Lord.*

His Father said, But it is written, It is God which worketh in you both to will and to do of His good pleasure. In My servant Paul I wrought an earnest expectation and a hope that in nothing he should be ashamed, but that always Christ should be magnified in his body. I am the God of thine expectation and thy hope.

*His thoughts said, But I am not St. Paul.*

His Father said, Hast thou watched a wave fill a shell on the shore? Thou art My shell. I am the God of thy hope. Wave upon wave I will flow over thee, poor empty shell that thou art. With all joy and peace I will fill thee, and thou shalt abound in hope.

*His thoughts said, What of those whom I love and long to help but cannot?*

His Father said, Am I a God at hand, and not a God afar off? Am I not with them, My child? Thou knowest that I am.

. . . . . .

How often we have been tempted to wish that we could shelter one and another, Indian and foreign too, from hurting things, especially from the long ache of battle-wounds. Vain wish and foolish. We never can. We can only watch, as perhaps their angels watch while they go through everything, more than conquerors by the grace of the Conqueror.

*His thoughts said, I cannot go on any longer.*

His Father said, Thou canst. Thou canst do all things I appoint, through Christ which strengtheneth thee. Doth the burning sun distress thee? There shall be a shadow from the heat. Art thou beaten by the storm? There shall be a covert for thee from storm and from rain. Dost thou say with another servant of Mine, 'My daily furnace is the tongue of men'? Thou knowest how to find thy way to the Pavilion, where thou shalt be kept from the strife of tongues. Or is it that thou art too weary to know why thou art so weary? Then come unto Me and I will refresh thee.

> Heart that is weary because of the way,
> Facing the wind and the sting of the spray,
> Come unto Me, and I will refresh you.

> Heart that has tasted of travail and toil,
> Burdened for souls whom the foe would despoil,
> Come unto Me, and I will refresh you.

> Heart that is frozen — a handful of snow,
> Heart that is faded — a sky without glow,
> Come unto Me, and I will refresh you.

> Heart that is weary, O come unto Me,
> Fear not, whatever the trouble may be,
> Come unto Me, and I will refresh you.

K 91

## The Shell

Upon the sandy shore an empty shell,
  Beyond the shell infinity of sea;
O Saviour, I am like that empty shell,
  Thou art the Sea to me.

A sweeping wave rides up the shore, and lo,
  Each dim recess the coilèd shell within
Is searched, is filled, is filled to overflow
  By water crystalline.

Not to the shell is any glory then:
  All glory give we to the glorious sea.
And not to me is any glory when
  Thou overflowest me.

Sweep over me Thy shell, as low I lie;
  I yield me to the purpose of Thy will,
Sweep up, O conquering waves, and purify
  And with Thy fulness fill.

TJ 68

64

## Lulla

Her name was Lulla. She was five years old, a Brahman child of much promise. She had sickened suddenly with an illness which we knew from the first must be dangerous. We could not ask a medical missionary to leave his hospital, a day and a half distant, for the sake of one child, but we did the best we could. We sent an urgent message to a medical evangelist trained at Neyyoor, who lived nearer, and he came at once. He arrived an hour too late.

But before he came we had seen this. It was in that chilly hour between night and morning. A lantern burned dimly in the room where Lulla lay; there was nothing in that darkened room to account for what we saw. The child was in pain, struggling for breath, turning to us for what we could not give. I left her with Mabel Wade and Ponnamal, and, going to a side room, cried to our Father to take her quickly.

I was not more than a minute away, but when I returned she was radiant. Her little lovely face was lighted with amazement and happiness. She was looking up and clapping her hands as delighted children do. When she saw me she stretched out her arms and flung them round my neck, as though saying Good-bye, in a hurry to be gone; then she turned to the others in the same eager way, and then again, holding out her arms to Someone whom we could not see, she clapped her hands.

Had only one of us seen this thing, we might have doubted. But we all three saw it. There was no trace of pain in her face. She was never to taste of pain again. We saw nothing in that dear child's face but unimaginable delight.

We looked where she was looking, almost thinking that we should see what she saw. What must the fountain of joy be if the spray from the edge of the pool can be like that? When we turned the next bend of the road, and the sorrow that waited there met us, we were comforted, words cannot tell how tenderly, by this that we had seen when we followed the child almost to the border of the Land of Joy . . . it was as though a hand drew back a corner of the curtain that hangs between our world and that other where forces move to direct our tangled and painful affairs.

GC 129

## The tamarind tree

When in 1914 Ponnammal, our first to enter into the Joy of the Lord, was on her way thither, she lay for weeks in a room close by two young tamarind trees. They grew in what was then a patch of dry ground. Often she spoke of those trees. She seemed to see the work, then so young, under the form of a tamarind tree. . . . The seed of the tamarind is a little polished brown bean, so small, so inconspicuous, that one might drop a seed out of a handful and not miss it, and without knowing it, sow a forest.

It was something like that when this tamarind tree was sown. Nobody knew that a seed had been dropped till a little tree appeared where there had been no green thing before, but only dry ground. . . .

At first, while this new little thing was beginning to grow, we were continually out in camp, and purposely had very few belongings. But later we had to make home for the children, and that meant room for books. So books began to come. . . .

It is delightful to come upon family affinities, and even a family likeness, such as we found in the Bavarian Sturmi; as for the Dutchman, Gerard Groote, who lived in the fourteenth century, he seems to belong to us or we to him in a special way. For it was he who gave us our name for the Sisters of the Common Life, without whom the work which has grown, as Ponnammal would say, into a tree with wide-spreading branches, could never have grown at all. . . .

Gerard Groote's Brothers and Sisters of the Common Life broke free from the trammels of those days. They mingled freely in the world for purposes of service, spread abroad good reading, worked hard, did not beg, taught the people and especially the children, wore simple clothes, followed a simple manner of life.

TMS 270

## Sisters of the Common Life

We had at that time seven Indian girls who were seeking to live a life of unreserved devotion, a life without fences. . . . Something was required to unite and fortify them. . . . We shaped ourselves into a group and called ourselves 'Sisters of the Common Life'. . . . The name came from the Brotherhood of Common Life, founded by Gerard Groote, of Holland. The Brothers worked with their hands and gave themselves to the training of 'such as sought, apart from the evil about them, a pure and godly life.' Communion with God and laborious work filled their days. They lived the common life, but they lived it with God for men. Our thought in taking the name was that the line so often drawn between spiritual and secular has no place with us if we follow Him who not only withdrew to the mountain, but also went about doing good.

Our meetings were mainly in English. Except our Bible and the *Pilgrim's Progress,* there were no books in Tamil that offered just what these girls began to want. Rolle and Suso and Tersteegen, on whom the still dews fell in the century of turmoil that we think of as Tamerlane's, and Bishop Moule and Josephine Butler of our own time, and Thomas à Kempis, pupil of Groote and Brother of Common Life, Samuel Rutherford and Père Didon, brothers in spirit though divided by the letter of the law, and the brave and burning souls of every age, these had left torches.

This group of girls has grown steadily year by year as one and another, drawn by the irresistible cords of love, have come asking to join it.

They have meant much to the Fellowship, whose ministry includes the care of and dealing with many different characters. Some of the children are from the best stock of India, but some have everything against them . . . there are various races in our family, and there are many castes. Nothing but the love of God can control and fuse into happy unity such diversity as this, and all have not yielded to the love of God. The unyielding can greatly exercise the patience of those who have to do with them; they send us again and again to the God of hope for renewals in hope.

But perhaps only one who has had to guide a work which is continuous (that is, without free spaces such as school and college offer) and which is always demanding more and more spiritual energy, can fully appreciate what it is to have such fellow-workers as these in the centre of things. Is there something to be done from which the flesh shrinks? 'Ask her, she is a Sister of the Common Life. She will do it.'

We soon gathered much lovely star-dust such as Raymond Lull's well known saying about the Moorish battlefield: 'It appears to me that victory can be won in no other way than Thou, O Lord Christ, with Thy apostles didst seek to win it, by love and prayer, by shedding of tears and blood, by self-sacrifice, by spiritual not by carnal weapons.' And Rutherford's from his prison in Aberdeen: 'Why should I start at the plough of my Lord, that maketh deep furrows on my soul? He purposeth a crop.' And Thomas à Kempis' calm word from his cell: 'Blessed are the single-hearted; for they shall enjoy much peace.'

'This sacred work demands, not lukewarm, selfish, slack souls, but hearts more finely tempered then steel, wills purer and harder than the diamond.' Père Didon gave us that, and Bishop Bardsley this: 'When a soul sets out to find God it does not know whither it will come and by what path it will be led; but those who catch the vision are ready to follow the Lamb whithersoever He goeth, regardless of what that following may involve for them. And it is as they follow, obedient to what they have seen, in this spirit of joyful adventure that their path becomes clear before them, and they are given the power to fulfil their high calling. They are those who have the courage to break conventionalities, who care not at all what the world thinks of them because they are entirely taken up with the tremendous realities of the soul and God.'

'*The Cross is the attraction.*' This was one of our words from the first. For 'the symbol of the Christian Church is not a burning bush nor a dove, nor an open book, nor a halo round a submissive head, nor a crown of splendid honour. It is a Cross.' (C. M. Clow)

These and other true things we read together and then very simply wrote:

*My Vow.*
Whatsoever Thou sayest unto me, by Thy grace I will do it.
*My Constraint.*
Thy love, O Christ, my Lord.
*My Confidence.*
Thou art able to keep that which I have committed unto Thee.
*My Joy.*
To do Thy will, O God.
*My Discipline.*
That which I would not choose, but which Thy love appoints.
*My Prayer.*
Conform my will to Thine.
*My Motto.*
Love to live: Live to love.
*My Portion.*
The Lord is the portion of mine inheritance.

Teach us, good Lord, to serve Thee more faithfully; to give and not to count the cost; to fight and not to heed the wounds; to toil and not to seek for rest; to labour and not to ask for any reward, save that of knowing that we do Thy will, O Lord our God.

Between twenty and thirty girls have signed this confession of love since that first evening, March 18, 1916. Of these, several have married, for it is always understood that obedience to their Lord's 'whatsoever' may lead to that. Some are out in the villages, some are here.

GC 158

## Under the tree

Upon a day when anxieties were pressing on all sides, I sat through a hot afternoon under a tree by the wayside, waiting for a bullock-cart which had somehow wandered and left me stranded.

Cloud and mist shadowed the hills, but overhead there was blazing blue, and the tree offered little shade. Its friendliness lay in its great trunk, which made an armchair, and sitting on the ground there, I waited.

It was the kind of day the Psalmist had in mind when he wrote about the multitude of his thoughts within him. For a fear had begun to move in us. What if the one whom we very sorely needed [Ponnammal] was not recovering, but slowly dying? How could we go on without her? I had been helping her Prèmie Sittie (Frances Beath) to nurse her in hospital, and was now needed at home to relieve Arulai Tara, who was beginning to be worn out with over-many burdens. What if she broke? Then we should have no one able to undertake responsibility to help with all these children.

And there were little ones for whose sake we were fighting, but, as it seemed, in vain, and everything looked almost impossible, though, thank God, the thought of giving up never came. But questions did: Shall the throne of iniquity have fellowship with Thee? Why do these things happen, O Lord God of the spirits of all flesh? And this grief, this mist of grief, must it fall in rain?

Presently, as I sat there, words began to sing themselves over to me:

> Far in the future lieth a fear,
> Like a long, low mist of grey,
> Gathering to fall in dreary rain,
> Thus doth thy heart within thee complain;

And even now thou art afraid, for round thy dwelling
The flying winds are ever telling
Of the fear that lieth grey,
Like a gloom of brooding mist upon the way.

But the Lord is always kind,
Be not blind
To the shining of His face,
To the comforts of His grace.
Hath He ever failed thee yet?
Never, never. Wherefore fret?
O fret not thyself, nor let thy heart be troubled,
Neither let it be afraid.

The second verse left the mist and rain behind: 'Wake the voice of joy and health within thy dwelling,' was the word now.

The verses appeared to be rather formless, but they were consoling, and to write them down helped through that scorching hour. The only paper at hand was the thin, cheap, brown paper of our Indian bazaars. It was wrapped round a spirits-of-wine bottle which I was taking home. One could not peel the paper off, it was too thin for that, it stuck like skin to the glass; so the writing had to wind round the bottle. It was not a tidy effort, but 'When you cannot do what you want to do, do something else' is among the smaller harbour-lights by which we steer, and when this 'something else' was finished the wandering bullock-cart trundled up with a gallant jingle of bells, the bottle and I climbed into the cart, and an hour or so later were home.

There immediately crowds of things rushed up and I forgot about the words on the bottle. Nor had I meant them to be kept. They did not seem worth that. But someone retrieved them and another set them to music, so they have survived. And never again on any journey on an Indian road did I pass a tree buttressed in this particular way without being reminded of that day and that comfort.

I have told of it — so very small a thing to tell at all when one considers what great things are happening in the world — because it may be that there are other roads in other lands and streets in many a town set with reminders of times which, if only we would let them remind us, would say, 'There, by that turning, as you went into that shop, as you saw that building, or that tree by the wayside, in the multitude of the sorrows that you had in your heart, the comforts of your God refreshed your soul. Fear not therefore, for He who was with you then is with you now.' And perhaps the story of my tree may recall to some reader a forgotten consolation.

For He who is the Strength of our heart, and our Portion for ever, does not weary of repeating the words that repetition can only make the more beloved. And He often uses common things — even the trunk of a tree — to recall the music of those words.

K 35

O Lord, my heart is all a prayer,
  But it is silent unto Thee;
I am too tired to look for words,
  I rest upon Thy sympathy
To understand when I am dumb;
  And well I know Thou hearest me.

I know Thou hearest me because
  A quiet peace comes down to me,
And fills the places where before
  Weak thoughts were wandering wearily;
And deep within me it is calm,
  Though waves are tossing outwardly.

GC 54

75

### About the death of Ponnammal

It is not by giving us back what He has taken that our Lord teaches us His deepest lessons, but by patiently waiting beside us till we can say: I accept the will of my God as good and acceptable and perfect, for loss or for gain. This, word for word, spelled out by Ponnammal's death-bed, was the lesson set to us to learn:

He said, 'I will forget the dying faces;
The empty places,
They shall be filled again.
O voices mourning deep within me, cease.'
But vain the word; vain, vain;
*Not in forgetting lieth peace.*

He said, 'I will crowd action upon action,
The strife of faction
Shall stir me and sustain;
O tears that drown the fire of manhood, cease.'
But vain the word; vain, vain;
*Not in endeavour lieth peace.*

He said 'I will withdraw me and be quiet,
Why meddle in life's riot?
Shut be my door to pain.
Desire, thou dost befool me, thou shalt cease.'
But vain the word; vain, vain;
*Not in aloofness lieth peace.*

He said, 'I will submit; I am defeated.
God hath depleted
My life of its rich gain.
O futile murmurings, why will ye not cease?'
But vain the word; vain, vain;
*Not in submission lieth peace.*

76

He said, 'I will accept the breaking sorrow
Which God tomorrow
Will to His son explain.'
Then did the turmoil deep within him cease.
*Not vain the word, not vain;*
*For in acceptance lieth peace.*

GC 111;   TJ 40

## Passages on the life of the spirit

Most of us find ourselves at times in the midst of the Valley where the pilgrim had to walk, where, ever and anon, flame and smoke come out in abundance, with sparks and hideous noises, things that care not for our sword. And there are doleful voices there, and rushings to and fro, and all this goes on for several miles together. But if we use the weapon called *All prayer* (praying when we feel most prayerless, for 'God accepteth the good-will and the travail of His servant, howsoever we feel') and if we walk on in the strength of the Lord God, those fiends of the Valley will give back and come no further.

PU 28

To look up into a dark sky and see it suddenly open, as lightning plays across it, to see in one revealing flash deep into the kingdoms of light, is to know what prayer most truly is. There is mystery, but beyond that darkness is not a deeper darkness, but light — kingdoms of light.

PU 29

How can any, we often wonder, bear up through the fears and the desolations of life without rock underfoot? Not to be sure of whom we have believed, or of what we have believed, must be like standing on quicksand with a blinding scurry of mist about one, and no clear air overhead.

PU 79

## Abundantly satisfied

PSALM 36.8. *Abundantly satisfied.*

This is meant to be our word always, however things are. Human happiness depends on circumstances — health,

78

freedom from care, joy of being together, work we love, power to do it, and so on. Divine happiness is quite different. It depends on none of these things. It is written that through much tribulation we enter into the Kingdom of God. Ease of any sort was never promised. It seems to me that we are often called to live a double life: in much tribulation (when we think of the poor world); and yet, in the deepest places of our souls, *abundantly satisfied* — and therefore, in peace ourselves, and able to help others to be peaceful.

EW 58

## The spirit of love

2 TIMOTHY 1.7. In Tamil we have a polite word, which tells someone who asks for something, that we have nothing to give; we have run short of it — *Poochiam*.

One day I felt like saying *Poochiam* about love. I had run short of it. I was in the Forest, and I had just read a letter which was hard to answer lovingly. I was sitting by The Pool at the time, and presently began to watch the water flow down through the deep channel worn in the smooth rocks above it. There was always inflow, so there was always outflow. Never for one minute did the water cease to flow in, and so never for one moment did it cease to flow out; and I knew, of course, that the water that flowed out was the water that flowed in. The hollow that we call The Pool had no water of its own, and yet all the year round there was an overflow.

*God hath not given you the spirit of fear . . . but of love.*

If love flows in, love will flow out. Let love flow in. That was the word of the pool. There is no need for any of us to run short of love. We need never say *Poochiam.*

EW 172

## Discipline

There was a day, near the close of 1916, while the depression of the War was heavy upon us all, when the future of the work rose up and frightened me. My heart sank. I knew that I must ask for something to brace the slack fibres, and when a call for a new decision of faith came and I could not rise to it, the deadly truth had me in its grip: I was afraid. Of what use is a frightened soldier in battle?

But God hath not given the spirit of fear, but of power and love and of discipline. *Discipline* — the word was like the sting of cold rain in the face. This flabbiness was not faith. How recover? How be renewed in the spirit of the mind? Lord, do something, do anything. Bid me come to Thee from any boat on any water, only teach me how to walk on the sea. There was no answer that I heard for a while. Then, suddenly, and with complete unexpectedness, came a word in the ear.

It is not necessary to write that word; to each apart is his discipline.

GC 157

## The little Christian girl

Everyone knows how often help given to a child is a key to the parents' hearts. But there are some who come to us too late. And yet there is something that can be done. Prayer can follow. This is a story of succour to a little Christian girl who lived a day's journey from Dohnavur. She was sent to us by a fellow-missionary who had hoped that we could do something; to hear her story is like looking through a window into a truly Christian home. The story begins sadly enough, for the child was dying of inoperable cancer, and her father took her away. After her death the friend who had sent her to us wrote to our doctor:

> For the last five days she had no pain and she insisted on getting up on her feet and with her father's help she walked about the house. For those five days she knew that she would go home on the fifth day at three o'clock. The Lord had told her so, and she was full of joy; so our prayers for peace and trust were answered abundantly above what we asked, for she was even merry. She longed to go to the beautiful place ready for her, and was impatient of being delayed by fond parents. She made them promise to be cheerful and not grieve, and said they must give her up willingly to the Lord.
>
> She sang many hymns and laughed at her father for singing in wrong time and sang for him. She said many verses, especially Psalm 23, and was glad and happy, and comforting all her friends up to the last fifteen minutes.
>
> The parents cannot grieve. They are full of wonder at God's doing; so the mystery of such suffering for a child is to some extent solved. She is a witness once more that Christ tasted death for every man.
>
> When she walked round the house, her idea was a journey. As Christian had been told, so she had been told to be ready, and she declared that she must walk all the way home, and

that was why she was so happy when she was walking; she was really (she felt) on her way home.

There must be many who have been compelled to leave someone to suffer and die, perhaps in circumstances that seemed to forbid peace and, how much more, joy. Thinking of such, we let this story give its cupful of sweet solace. For it is comforting that we have a Saviour who is equal to any kind of forbidding circumstance, even the death by cancer of a little child.

GC 292

## Light and dark

We are up on the rock-top still, resting in the utter peace. The sun has set. It will soon be after-glow. The plain looks immense in the gloaming, the mountains very high. Five minutes pass. We watch the clouds slip down the bare slopes of the nearer hills. There is a hush as if mountains, plain and sky were waiting for something sure to come. It comes, gently at first, then with a majestic sweep as the pent-up energy of light breaks forth and floods the atmosphere. Then the sky flames out in a fan of fire, and the russet reaches of burnt hill grass, and the patches of reddish earth on the plain, kindle suddenly, and the mountains half emerging from clouds that are golden now, stand solemn in their purple. All the world seems full of song, with shapes and colours for music and words, as the sky grows blue in the east, and pales into opal above. To the west it still burns and flames, and the glory of it lingers on the plain as we come down. We almost quite forget the dark in this loveliness of light.

But it is there: we see it personified, down below. For set in a hollow, jutting jet black from the black of the shadow, with outstretched hand that grasps a knife, is a single hateful threatening form, the idol of the rock.

OJ 228

83

## My Quietness

O Thou who art my quietness, my deep repose,
My rest from strife of tongues, my holy hill,
Fair is Thy pavilion, where I hold me still.
Back let them fall from me, my clamorous foes,
Confusions multiplied;
From crowding things of sense I flee, and in
   Thee hide.
Until this tyranny be overpast,
Thy hand will hold me fast;
What though the tumult of the storm increase,
Grant to Thy servant strength, O Lord, and bless
   with peace.

TJ 2

## How 'If' came to be written

One evening a fellow-worker brought me a trouble about a younger one who was missing the way of Love. This led to a wakeful night, for the word at such times is always, 'Lord, is it I? Have I failed her anywhere? What do I know of Calvary Love?' And then sentence by sentence the 'Ifs' came, almost as if spoken aloud to the inward ear.

Next morning they were shared with another (for they had been written down in pencil in the night), and then a few others shared. After this some copies were printed on our little hand-press for the Dohnavur Fellowship only; and that led to this booklet. . . .

Some of the 'Ifs' appear to be related to pride, selfishness, or cowardice, but digging deeper we come upon an unsuspected lovelessness at the root of them all. . . .

I have felt these words scorching to write, but it is borne upon me that in spite of all our hymns and prayers (so many of them for love), it is possible to be content with the shallows of love, if indeed such shallows should be called love at all.

The more we ponder our Lord's words about love, and the burning words the Spirit gave to His followers to write, the more acutely do we feel our deadly lack. The Searchlight of the Spirit discovers us to ourselves, and such a discovery leaves us appalled. How can even He who is the God of all patience have patience with us? Like Job we abhor ourselves and repent in dust and ashes.

IF v, 70

## If

If I am perturbed by the reproach and misunderstanding that may follow action taken for the good of souls for whom I must give account, if I cannot commit the matter and go on in peace and in silence, remembering Gethsemane and the Cross, then I know nothing of Calvary love.

If I can hurt another by speaking faithfully without much preparation of spirit, and without hurting myself far more than I hurt that other, then I know nothing of Calvary love.

If I hold on to choices of any kind, just because they are my choice; if I give any room to my private likes and dislikes, then I know nothing of Calvary love.

If I am soft to myself and slide comfortably into the vice of self-pity and self-sympathy; if I do not by the grace of God practise fortitude, then I know nothing of Calvary love.

If I cannot in honest happiness take the second place (or the twentieth); if I cannot take the first without making a fuss about my unworthiness, then I know nothing of Calvary love.

If I take offence easily, if I am content to continue in a cool unfriendliness, though friendship be possible, then I know nothing of Calvary love.

If a sudden jar can cause me to speak an impatient, unloving word, then I know nothing of Calvary love. (For a cup brimful of sweet water cannot spill even one drop of bitter water however suddenly jolted.)

If the care of a soul (for a community) be entrusted to me, and I consent to subject it to weakening influences, because the voice of the world — my immediate Christian world — fills my ears, then I know nothing of Calvary love.

If monotony tries me, and I cannot stand drudgery; if stupid people fret me and little ruffles set me on edge; if I make much of the trifles of life, then I know nothing of Calvary love.

If interruptions annoy me, and private cares make me

impatient; if I shadow the souls about me because I myself am shadowed, then I know nothing of Calvary love.

If souls can suffer alongside, and I hardly know it, because the spirit of discernment is not in me, then I know nothing of Calvary love.

If I become entangled in any 'inordinate affection'; if things or places or people hold me back from obedience to my Lord, then I know nothing of Calvary love.

If the praise of man elates me and his blame depresses me; if I cannot rest under misunderstanding without defending myself; if I love to be loved more than to love, to be served more than to serve, then I know nothing of Calvary love.

If I do not forget about such a trifle as personal success, so that it never crosses my mind, or if it does, is never given a moment's room there; if the cup of spiritual flattery tastes sweet to me, then I know nothing of Calvary love.

If I slip into the place that can be filled by Christ alone, making myself the first necessity to a soul instead of leading it to fasten upon Him, then I know nothing of Calvary love.

If my interest in the work of others is cool; if I think in terms of my own special work; if the burdens of others are not my burdens too, and their joys mine, then I know nothing of Calvary love.

If I wonder why something trying is allowed, and press for prayer that it may be removed; if I cannot be trusted with any disappointment, and cannot go on in peace under any mystery, then I know nothing of Calvary love.

# 1931 — 1951

In 1931, on a visit to the town
which she called Joyous City,
Amma had a serious accident which was to
change the whole course of her life.
Thereafter she was confined to her room,
and was unable to take part in the physical
activities of the Dohnavur Fellowship.
She was in constant pain, and out of this
arose some of her most helpful
reflections on the problem of suffering
and the meaning of the Cross.

## Another Shall Gird Thee

Are these the days when thou dost gird thyself
And walkest where thou wouldest, battle days,
Crowded and burdened and yet lit with praise,
Days of adventure; eager, glorious choice
Folded in every hour? Rejoice, rejoice,
    O happy warrior, if so it be,
    For surely thou shalt see
Jesus Himself draw near and walk with thee.

Or doth another gird thee, carry thee
Whither thou wouldest not, and doth a cord
Bind hand and foot, and flying thought and word?
An enemy hath done it, even so,
(Though why that power was his thou dost not know)
    O happy captive, fettered and yet free,
    Believe, believe to see
Jesus Himself draw near and walk with thee.

So either way is blessed; either way
Leadeth unto the Land of Heart's Desire;
Thy great Companion's love can never tire;
He is thy Confidence, He is thy Song;
Let not thy heart be troubled, but be strong,
    O happy soul, to whom is given to see
    On all the roads that be,
Jesus Himself draw near and walk with thee.

TJ 86

## Second causes — Persian carpets

In a letter of Samuel Rutherford's dated 1640, he speaks about the difficulty of being patient if we stay our thoughts 'down among the confused rollings and wheels of second causes; as, Oh the place! Oh the time! Oh if this had not been, this had not followed! Oh the linking of this accident with this time and place! Look up to the master-motion and the first wheel.'

If this had not been, this had not followed — how exactly true to life. The temptation to think along these lines can be vinegar upon nitre. That day, now over a year ago, when we four happy people found the little low door leading into the courtyard of the house we had rented in Joyous City locked, we stood outside wondering what we should do. The old man who had charge of the key was not there, and the key was not to be found.

So we stood in the swiftly gathering twilight, ready to turn contentedly and go home if we could not get in. Just then another old man hurried up, the huge key of his own courtyard door in his hands. 'This may open it,' he said hopefully; there was a minute's fumbling, the door opened, and we went in. If the old man had not hurried up with a key? If the door had not opened? The confused rollings and wheels of second causes do not help us much here, or anywhere. The Lord allowed it. Therefore, so far as we are concerned, He did it. Himself hath done it. And all He does is good. And what a special kindness to allow a disablement to come in the direct line of duty — we thank Thee, O Father.

There is another word in Rutherford's Letters which often helps: 'They who contend with Zion see not what He is doing when they are set to work, as undersmiths or servants, to the work of refining the saints. Satan's hand also, by them, is at the melting of the Lord's vessels of mercy, and their office in God's house is to scour and cleanse vessels for the King's table.'

The coolies who dug the pit where no pit was supposed to be, the old man who did not leave the key in its right place and so caused delay till dusk turned to dark, were the undersmiths, and all the troubles that followed were only scullions cleansing and scouring together for good.

But there are limits set to the activities of the smiths and the scullions. On October 6 a member of our Fellowship who was in prayer in London, was suddenly caused to feel that danger was threatening the one here who, eighteen days afterwards, fell into that pit in the dark. He prayed, not the easy prayer of the unconcerned, but the prayer of the greatly burdened. There was a sense of fear upon him, as of a terror by night. Then peace came, and he knew that his prayer was heard. And these who have tended the months know that such a fall might have been far more serious in its effect. The least, not the greatest, harm it could have done was allowed. But that was not all. Four or five hours later, as the motor-lorry with its cargo of the whole and maimed was on its way to Neyoor in the black night, in torrents of rain on a flooded road built up between rice-fields and water, it crossed a deep fissure caused by the washing away of part of the road, where a tree had been torn up by the roots and flung down the steep bank.

The lorry was going at such speed that it had no time to sink into the hole; all of us were for a moment tossed like balls, and the injured limb in its splints, jerked out of the hand that held it, came down on the lorry-floor with a thud. These rifts are often of unknown depth and extent and can be dangerous. Only the angels, and the Lord of the angels, who had set a skilled hand at the wheel, saved it from plunging into the rice-field, just then a swamp, or the deep water on the other side. If the lorry had gone over either unprotected edge it would almost certainly have turned as it fell, and we should have been drowned or smothered in mud.

But it did not go over the edge. And yet if it had? Should we

92

have said that prayer was not answered? It is a petty view of our Father's love and wisdom which demands or expects an answer according to our desires, apart from His wisdom. We see hardly one inch of the narrow lane of time. To our God eternity lies open as a meadow. It must seem strange to the heavenly people who have seen the beautiful End of the Lord, that we should ever question what Love allows to be, or ever call a prayer 'unanswered' when the answer is not what we expect; as one of our baby-songs says, 'Isn't No an answer?' And where what is called a fatal accident is concerned I feel like adding, 'Isn't heaven an answer?'

RB 160

## Facing the future

There was one who was not afraid of any evil tidings, for her heart stood fast believing in the Lord. And her trust was in the tender mercy of God for ever and ever.

Often He had arisen as light in the darkness.

Often she had called upon Him in troubles and He had delivered her, and heard her say what time the storm fell upon her. He had been merciful, loving and righteous, and she had said, 'Who is like unto the Lord our God, that hath His dwelling so high; and yet humbleth Himself to behold the things that are in heaven and earth?' And now she found herself standing alone, looking into a great mist.

Fold after fold the hills lay there before her, but always in mist. She could see no path, except a little track in the valley below. She thought that she was quite alone, and for a while she stood looking, listening, and feeling this loneliness and uncertainty harder to bear than any acute distress had ever been.

Then, softly, voices began to speak within her, now discouraged, now encouraging.

'My flesh and my heart faileth.'

'But God is the strength of my heart and my portion for ever.'

'My lovers and my friends stand aloof from my soul; and my kinsmen stand afar off.'

'Nevertheless, I am continually with Thee: Thou hast holden me by my right hand.'

'My tears have been my meat day and night; while they continually say unto me, Where is thy God?'

'Thou shalt answer for me, O Lord my God.'

'Why art thou cast down, O my soul? and why art thou disquieted within me?'

'Hope thou in God; for I shall yet praise Him who is the health of my countenance, and my God.'

'My way is hidden from my God.'

'He knoweth the way that I take. All my ways are before Him. As for God, His way is perfect and He maketh my way perfect. They thirsted not when He led them through the deserts. Will they faint when He leads them through the hills?'

Then she looked again at the mist, and it was lightening, and she knew that she was not alone, for her God was her refuge and strength, a very present help in trouble. He was about her path; He would make good His loving-kindness toward her, and His loving-kindness was comfortable. Nor could she fear any more, for those dim folds in the hills were open ways to Him. He would not let her be disappointed of her hope.

So it was enough for her to see only the next few steps, because He would go before her and make His footsteps a way to walk in. And of this she was also sure: *He whom she followed saw through the mist to the end of the way.* She would never be put to confusion.

And in that hour a song was given to her. She sang it as she walked: 'O what great troubles and adversities hast Thou showed me! And yet didst Thou turn and refresh me: and broughtest me up from the deep of the earth again. The Lord is my Strength and my Shield; my heart trusted in Him, and I am helped; therefore my heart danceth for joy, and in my song will I praise Him. Thou drewest near in the day that I called upon Thee: Thou saidst, Fear not. O Lord, Thou hast pleaded the causes of my soul; Thou hast redeemed my life. O let my mouth be filled with Thy praise, that I may sing of Thy glory and honour all the day long, *for Thou, Lord, hast never failed them that seek Thee.'*

And as she walked thus and sang, others whom she did not see because of the mist that still lay on her way, heard her singing and were comforted and helped to follow on, even unto the end.

FT 7

### Accepting the will of God

To accept the will of God never leads to the miserable feeling
that it is useless to strive any more. God does not ask for the
dull, weak, sleepy acquiescence of indolence. He asks for
something vivid and strong. He asks us to co-operate with
Him, actively willing what He wills, our only aim His glory.
To accept in this sense is to come with all the desire of the
mind unto the place which the Lord shall choose, and to
minister in the name of the Lord our God *there* — not
otherwise. *Where the things of God are concerned,
acceptance always means the happy choice of mind and heart
of that which He appoints, because (for the present) it is His
good and acceptable and perfect will.*

. . . . . .

Unreserved acceptance opens the way for the turning of the
captivity — 'whoso offereth thanksgiving glorifieth Me and
prepareth a way that I may show him the salvation of God.'

GM 31

### Illness and prayer

I have not found myself that illness makes prayer easier, nor do
any of our family who have been ill tell me that they have
found it so. Prayerfulness does not seem to be a flower of the
spirit that grows of itself. When we are well perhaps we rather
take it for granted that it does, as though what is sometimes
called a 'sick-bed' offered natural soil for that precious flower. I
do not think that it does. A bed can be a place of dullness of
spirit as well as of body, and prayer is, after all, work — the
most strenuous work in all the world. And yet it is our only
way of joining the fighting force. So what can we do about it?
    One night, soon after neuritis had taken possession of me
from shoulder-blade to finger-tips, I could no more gather

myself up to pray than I could turn in bed without the help of the Lotus Bud, who was my faithful night-nurse. But I could read, and I opened on Psalm 109.

*Do Thou for me, O God the Lord.* Do what? It does not say. It just says, *Do Thou for me.*

And the prayer, so simple, so easy for a tired heart, had a delivering power. It delivered from the oppression of the enemy. 'Now there was leaning on Jesus' bosom one of His disciples, whom Jesus loved'; it was like that.

And soon the prayer passed into the most restful kind of intercession, the only kind the ill can attain unto, for they cannot pray in detail and they may know little or nothing of the needs of their dearest. But He knows all, down to the smallest wish of the heart. So we do not need to coin our gold in words, we could not if we tried: we are far too tired for that; and He who knoweth our frame does not ask us to do anything so arduous: Do Thou for her, do Thou for him, do Thou for them, O God the Lord.

RB 53

### Fixed in pain

Very early on in the course of events I prayed for one and only one thing (leaving to my family all prayer for healing; this was different). I prayed that power to cover signs of pain might be given, so that no one coming into the room should be saddened. But the effort sometimes required to suppress those signs led to something unexpected. I had never before realised how terrible it must have been for our Saviour to be fixed in one position, and that position one which was intolerably agonising. He had not the help of movement, or of being moved.

It was, indeed, only a fraction of His piled-up suffering that was thus made vivid, but though it was only like a grain of the dust of that mountain, it was a real grain. The thought of it

97

sent me to read the Gospels again and again, and as I pondered that Atoning Sacrifice, the magnitude of the cost to the Father, who so loved that He gave Him, was made just a little clearer, and the blessed, adorable love of our Lord Jesus, who, through the Eternal Spirit, offered Himself (but who can fathom those words?) became more real too.

Will this reach one who does not know Him? Apart from Calvary, life is chaos, a confusion of distress, a black, deep horror of torment for all who are suffering severely, or who look through the thin skin of ice on the face of life to the black deeps below. To come to Him, the Supreme Sufferer, our Redeemer, to say to Him,

> Just as I am, without one plea
> But that Thy blood was shed for me,
> And that Thou bidd'st me come to Thee,
> O Lamb of God, I come,

is to find pardon, peace, heart rest. For the word is eternally true, *Come unto Me, all ye that labour and are heavy laden, and I will give you rest.*

> None other Lamb, none other Name,
> None other hope in heaven or earth or sea,
> None other hiding-place from guilt and shame,
>    None beside Thee.

> My faith burns low, my hope burns low;
> Only my heart's desire cries out in me
> By the deep thunder of its want and woe,
>    Cries out to Thee.

> Lord, Thou art life, though I be dead;
> Love's fire Thou art, however cold I be;
> Nor heaven have I, nor place to lay my head,
>    Nor home, but Thee.

These beautiful words, Christina Rossetti's, say all that I want to say.

## Pain

But to what end is pain? I do not clearly know. But I have noticed that when one who has not suffered draws near to one in pain there is rarely much power to help; there is not the understanding that leaves the suffering thing comforted, though perhaps not a word was spoken; and I have wondered if it can be the same in the sphere of prayer. Does pain accepted and endured give some quality that would otherwise be lacking in prayer? Does it create that sympathy which can lay itself alongside the need, feeling it as though it were personal, so that it is possible to do just what the writer of the Hebrews meant when he said, 'Remember them that are in bonds, *as bound with them;* and them which suffer adversity, *as being yourselves also in the body*'?

RB 125

## In Sleep

He gives to His beloved in sleep,
For when the spirit drifts from fields of time,
And wanders free in worlds remote, sublime,
    It meets Him there,
    The only Alone Fair.
    But were it bidden to tell
    The heavenly words that fell,
Dropping like sunlit rain through quiet air,
It could not, though it heard them everywhere.

Were some small fish in rock-pool close confined,
Swept in the backwash of a wave to sea,
Could it describe that blue immensity?
    Could the caged bird,
    Whose happy ear had heard
    The lark sing in high heaven,
    And had escaped, be bidden
To bind that rapture fast in earthly words?
Not so is bound the song of singing birds.

Nor can I tell what He gave me in sleep —
The mind, still conscious of the body's stress,
Hindered awhile, and in a wilderness
    I walked alone,
    Till One a long time known
    Drew near; 'Lord, may I come?
    For I would fain go Home.'
'Not yet, My child,' then waves on waves of blue,
Like the blue sea, or air that light pours through.

This is not much to bring of that land's gold,
But one word lingers of the shining dream,
'Be comforted, all ye who by a stream
        Watch wistfully,
        Lest your beloved be
        Swept to some shore unknown,
        All desolate, alone;
*It is not so, but now as heretofore,*
*The Risen Christ is standing on the shore.'*

TJ 50

## Rose from brier

*From thy brier shall blow a rose for others.*

All these letters* have been written that time the storm fell upon me, not after the coming of the calm. In the *Meditations* of Marcus Aurelius we are told that it is in our power to live free from all compulsion in the greatest tranquillity of mind, even if wild beasts tear in pieces the members of this kneaded matter which has grown around us. 'For what hinders the mind, in the midst of all this, from maintaining itself in tranquillity?' But when he wrote that, his kneaded matter was not being torn in pieces. It was sitting comfortably aloof from the claws of wild beasts; so his composure does not do much for us. It can, indeed, be exceedingly irritating. There is more of the pith of life in Satan's 'Put forth Thine hand now and touch his bone and his flesh' — we understand that.

> The toad beneath the harrow knows
> Exactly where each tooth-point goes;
> The butterfly upon the road
> Preaches contentment to that toad.

There can be minutes when the toad is not properly grateful to the butterfly — no, not even if he comes dressed like a very good Christian. He is upon the road: he isn't under the harrow; he never was there.

Such a minute came one morning when all I wanted was something which would help me to escape from myself; and there is nothing that can so quickly give this release as a book that takes me out of my own life into the lives of others.

Just then the post came — 'And a book packet!' said my dear nurse. Her voice with its note of expectation was as delightful

---

* Letters written originally to the Dohnavur Fellowship Invalids' League.

as what we hoped would be the contents of that parcel. Eagerly she opened it and eagerly I watched her. Would it be something like Bernard Allen's *Gordon and the Sudan,* which I had just read, or John Buchan's latest story? (No writer could carry me off to the heather just then as he could.) But no — that fat parcel was full of tracts for the sick. I tried those tracts, but somehow they took me nowhere. This sounds most unmissionary; unhappily, it is true. It was not till some time later, and after several similar experiences, that it struck me perhaps the reason was because they were obviously written by the well to the ill, to do them good; and so they could flutter past like ineffective butterflies. But I found that things written by those who were in pain themselves, or who had passed through pain to peace, like the touch of understanding in a dear human letter, did something that nothing except the words of our eternal Lord could ever do.

So these letters purposely go forth from under the harrow before the sharpness of the prod of a single tooth is forgotten.

RB 11

## Bird, butterfly, sunbird's nest

We have each our own private magic casement. The first glimpse of a snow mountain, or a stretch of purple heather, the tang of that same heather, the bitter-sweet scent of certain aromatic herbs, the sharp smell of seaweed, the soft breath of a meadow in clover, the sound of running waters, birds flying high in transparent blue, the first violet or primrose or patch of wood-sorrel, a cushion of ferny moss, a spray of wild rose — the heart knoweth its own casement. For some of us in Dohnavur it is just the whistle of the Malabar thrush.

This bird is a friend of rocks and rivers in deep woods, and when we go to our forest on the mountains, we know that the blissful moment between sleeping and waking of our first morning in that beloved place will thrill to the clear whistle just outside our windows, and we shall be caught away on the wings of a dream — whither? Who can tell? Only we know the casement is open and the air is golden and full of the flutings of a bird.

But it may be far from golden in the forest. It may be wild weather. Then slashing rain whips the low, tiled roof, and furious gusts tearing down the ravine threaten to uproot the houses that have dared to perch up there. The branches of the trees strike each other with a sound of loud complaining. Their leaves are colourless. A palm, thrusting through his lesser neighbours, tosses black plumes like ostrich feathers against the grey smear that is the sky. One such a morning a heavy gloom broods over the forest, a gloom like a pall. The place may be swept with cloud, or smothered in mist, and there may not be one cheerful thing to look at anywhere, except the log fire on the open hearth, and probably it smokes.

It may be a most melancholy morning, but nothing makes any difference to that bird. He whistles his inconsequent tune, never twice the same, never hurried; it is the most leisurely

104

thing imaginable. The key is continually changing (like life). You cannot follow him or ever anticipate him, you can only listen and love him.

And often in the crush of the common day on the Plains, or when a gloom has descended upon us — for not all days are sunny — we have thought of that brave bird who whistles through all weathers, and have thanked the God who made him, and asked Him to give us the courage of His bird.

For everywhere the perpetual endeavour of the enemy of souls is to discourage. If he can get the soul 'under the weather', he wins. It is not really what we go through that matters, it is what we go under that breaks us. We can bear anything if only we are kept inwardly victorious.

On a rainy day in the forest after the first burst of the monsoon is over, a surprising thing is often seen. The rain then is not the heaviest — that kind of rain comes down like solid grey walls of water or in great scourging rods — but it is as heavy as ordinary English rain: quite heavy enough, one would think, to destroy in a moment such a fragile thing as a butterfly.

And yet you may see the black-and-yellow *Papilio minos* of the forest out in the wet, hovering over the flowery bushes, lighting on one for a dripping moment, then fluttering off and across some open space. The spread of her wings is five or six inches from tip to tip; you watch half incredulously those five or six inches of delicate tissue borne down perhaps, sometimes, but always rising again, soaring again.

If God can make His birds to whistle in drenched and stormy darkness, if He can make His butterflies able to bear up under rain, what can He not do for the heart that trusts Him?

So there can never be anything to fear. Outside the room in Dohnavur where this book is being finished, a sunbird has hung her nest from a spray of valaris. The spray is as light as a spray of honeysuckle; and grows in much the same careless way. The nest is attached to the spray by a few threads of cobweb, but so delicately that the touch of a child would detach it; a cupful of water thrown at it would sweep it down. It is a mere nothing of a nest. But it took a week of patient mother-craft to make it. It is roofed, it has a porch, and set deep within is a bed of silky down.

We know now that we were foolish, but we could not help being anxious about the fate of that wee home; for our north-east monsoon was due, and the nest hung in the eye of the wind and beyond the eaves of the house. There was no shelter from the wind and the rain. And how would the tiny mother find her food in the weather that would soon be upon us? The father bird would feed her if he could, but in rain the convolvulus and other nectar-carrying flowers are dashed and sodden. How could those little jewels on wings survive, much less bring up a family? It seemed as if bird-wisdom for once were at fault.

The day the mother began to sit upon the two or three comfits that are her eggs, the monsoon broke. First came the wind; the spray swung from the branch and the nest swung from the spray. The wind did it no harm. Then the rain poured down in sheets; and still it swung in peace, for the four narrow leaves from whose axil the nest depended were so disposed that they turned into green gutters and carried off the water as quickly as it fell. Exactly where no rain could hurt it that nest hung, and the little mother sat calmly through those floods, her dainty head resting on the threshold of the porch which she had made on the south side — the sheltered side. If a drop of water fell on her long, curved beak, she sucked it up as though it had been honey. And always, somehow, she was fed.

I think to more than one of us the Father spoke then. There is something very precious about a little bird and her nest, but 'Ye are of more value than many sparrows — than many sunbirds.'

W 175

Think through me, Thoughts of God,
　My Father, quiet me,
Till in Thy holy presence, hushed,
　I think Thy thoughts with Thee.

Think through me, Thoughts of God,
　That always, everywhere,
The stream that through my being flows
　May homeward pass in prayer.

Think through me, Thoughts of God,
　And let my own thoughts be
Lost like the sand-pools on the shore
　Of the eternal sea.

TJ 75

107

## I am the God of the stars

[*From a letter written to a colleague at the time of Arulai's illness*]

I want you to have the comfort that was given to me a few nights ago. It was a night when all seemed too impossible to face. I went into my little side room and turned off the light lest any should see through the blind, and then at last drew back the blind (the curtain over the small window) and I looked out.

I saw a few stars through the trees. That was all.

Then as I sat there, wave upon wave came over me. I thought of so many of our beloved D.F.s, tired and getting near the end of the day's work, and others not very strong. How could the Family go on? I thought of the forces against it, some openly ill-wishers, some secretly so, and the one who would have stood like a rock through any storm and strengthened the hands of all, perhaps going from us, almost certainly going from us. How could we go on? And if we could not, or did not, what then? So much seemed to hang on so few. The line seemed a very thinly held line that night. And the grief and everything was just too much — till I looked again, looked up again, saw the stars. 'I am the God of the stars' — it was like a word spoken aloud in my ear. It was more than that.

At last I went out, this time to the bed you gave me, and I lay there and saw the stars more distinctly as there were fewer trees between, and again and again the word came, 'I am the God of the stars'. The little thing [*poem*] enclosed came later in the night. It only says a little of what those great words meant to me, but you will follow the thought.

> I am the God of the stars,
> They do not lose their way,
> Not one do I mislay,

Their times are in My Hand,
They move at My command.

I am the God of the stars,
Today as yesterday,
The God of thee and thine,
Less thine they are than Mine;
And shall Mine go astray?

I am the God of the stars,
Lift up thine eyes and see
As far as mortal may
Into Eternity;
And stay thy heart on Me.

Ask for me one thing if you hear that my child has passed on —
ask that I may not weaken, but strengthen those on whom the
heaviest burden falls. Ask for selflessness, power to help,
console, lift the edges of the burdens if I can't lift the whole.
Ask for love that forgets all but others.

ACD 356

## The death of Arulai

All who understand spiritual conflict, and what it means to
hold a long line on the edge of the enemy's country, will know
what the loss of even one in that thin line can be. There was
one among our Indian Sisters who was able, because of certain
gifts of insight and character and knowledge of Hindu ways of
thought, to succour souls caught in these black seas. In her
Bible I find this: 'The man who has no experience in the dark
has no secret to communicate in the light.' Perhaps these
words will show to the discerning what Arulai had to give, and
why we all felt that she was indeed impossible to spare. She had
never been strong, and, shortly before the Sisters of the

Common Life came into being, to give her the best chance of health that we could, we sent her in the hot weather to friends in the hills. She returned home far advanced in nephritis.

There came a day (it was our Prayer Day, but every day was a prayer day then) when, as I left her for an hour's wrestle with the fear that was now overshadowing us, a desperate kind of comfort came in the thought that she at least would never have to drink of this cup. The endurance of this pang (the rending of flesh from flesh) would never be asked of her, and somehow that did help. But we had to go further than that.

All that day she had been delirious, and she was still unconscious when I returned to the little side-room where one or other of us was with her night and day. And that night, when all was quiet, and when all human hope had fled, He to whom belong the issues from death came into the house, and took her by the hand, and called saying, Maid, arise.

But before this happened there had been time for a question and an answer. And again one instinctively turns to familiar words, because they tell so much better than mine could what I want to show: And behold there stood a man over against him with his sword drawn in his hand, and Joshua went unto him and said unto him, Art thou for us, or for our adversaries? (Lord, if Thou dost take Arulai, how can the work go on? Drive that question back to its root and how does it differ from Joshua's?) And he said, Nay; but as captain of the host of the Lord am I now come. And Joshua fell on his face to the earth, and did worship, and said unto him, What saith my Lord unto his servant?

And the captain of the Lord's host said unto Joshua, Loose thy shoe from off thy foot; for the place whereon thou standest is holy. And he did so.

And we did so too.

. . . In ways like this, in dealings which again and again touched the key people of our work, those precious ones who could never be replaced, we were taught that the disposal of His forces is wholly in the hands of our Commander-in-Chief. And it was in times like this that our nights became light about us.

GC 167

## Light in the Cell

*'And a light shined in the cell'*,
    And there was not any wall,
    And there was no dark at all,
Only Thou, Immanuel.

Light of Love shined in the cell,
    Turned to gold the iron bars,
    Opened windows to the stars,
Peace stood there as sentinel.

Dearest Lord, how can it be
    That Thou art so kind to me?
    Love is shining in my cell,
**Jesus, my Immanuel**.

TJ 114

112

## Tranquillity

One night, in the sudden way things happen here, a messenger ran into my room exclaiming, 'O Amma, Prémie Sittie and Arulai Accal [Frances Beath and Star] have returned safely, and they have brought Tranquillity!' And before I had time to do more than gasp, 'Tranquillity?' two arms were flung round my neck, a hot, wet face was crushed down upon mine, and a sobbing voice was murmuring all the love-words of the East in a torrent of grief and joy and affection; for it was Tranquillity, lost for twelve years.

Thirty years ago there were five little girls whose names were familiar to our friends: Arulai Tara, known as Star, Golden's daughter Perfection, Radiance, the Elf and her twin in age, whose name Tranquillity exactly fitted her.

Tranquillity was not in temple danger; like Arulai, Mimosa, the Brownie and others of those days, her heart had opened when first she heard of the love of our Lord Jesus Christ. Nothing her parents could do could hold her from Him, and at last they had allowed her to come to us. After her father's death she longed to comfort her mother and lead her to our Saviour. There were reasons which seemed to make a short visit home possible. Her brother and two aunts came to fetch her, and promised to bring her back within a week. As the bullock-cart turned through the gate into the village street, Tranquillity leaned out and waved her hand. That was our last glimpse of her for six months; and we had no letter from her or about her.

Then at last we traced her. It was in the days when motor-buses were only just beginning their activities, and as often as not they ran into a ditch or a tree, or sat down in the road and had to be tugged into port by bullocks. The faithful Pearl and I, who set forth in hopes of retrieving her, travelled chiefly by cart, partly by a wreck of a bus tied together with bits of rope, and at last arrived on foot at our destination, hot and tired, dusty and sticky.

It was a jungle village, and seemed full of shouting men and excited dogs. The thing we wanted most — a bath — was, of course, impossible; so was even one minute's quiet. We found Tranquillity, but she was not our Tranquillity. We saw a dull, dazed face, gentle as before, but with a lifeless gentleness. When we spoke of return with us, she froze. We took a meeting in that wild place that evening; men and women crowded round us, but no one seemed to be touched. The mother and aunts were hard. Tranquillity looked like a flower among them all, but a frozen flower.

That night we spread our mats on a verandah opening off the street, and the poor, half-starved dogs yelped and snarled round about us and all but on top of us, and the snores of sleepers filled any intervals left by the dogs. Next morning we sorrowfully left the place empty-handed. From that time on there was silence, till that amazing evening when she ran into my room like a wild thing.

And she was a wild thing when they found her, so Frances and Arulai say. They had been working in the *taluk* of Vishnu's-heaven, and had gone to the old Fort, to Mimosa's town, and to many other places, and they had traced Tranquillity. She had rushed out of her home when their bandy drove into the village, and, running up to them, she had cried out in joy, and then, turning to the people, 'See, my God has sent them!' For just at the time we had begun to plan this tour (we compared the date afterwards) a hunger of longing had seized her for Dohnavur, and for us and for all the life here stood for. She had prayed night and day, reminding her Father that she could not go alone, and asking that some one might be sent for her. Then she had a vivid dream. She was home again with us all, free once more. She had wept when she woke and found it was a dream, but she had taken courage to believe that it was from

God and meant that help was near, and she had told her people of her dream, and of her faith that God would send someone for her. Now, as she pointed to Frances and Arulai and said, 'See, my God has sent them!' they had nothing to say, for who can withstand a dream fulfilled? But our two could not stay; they promised if possible to return next day for her, and when the day passed and they did not come, she was sorely tempted to fear.

But she clung to her hope and to words of assurance which she read in the only Christian book her relations had allowed her to keep, probably because it looked like an English lesson-book. They did not know that it was made of undiluted Scripture, that pure ray from the Sun of Life, that strong meat of the soul. At last Frances and Arulai returned; and then seven green withs could not have bound her. So they brought her home, and here she was, haggard and wild indeed, but so happy that words failed her, and she wept what in our Indian speech we call eye-water of bliss. And with her was her little son.

When I heard the story of the twelve silent years, again, I wished, as I so often wish, that I could think in pictures across the sea. Nothing but flashing thought is alive enough for such a story; print strangles it.

Near to her village lives a magician who makes 'medicine' and charms, from the bodies of first-born babies. That medicine and a certain 'stroking' commonly used to influence the mind may have accounted for her state during the first few months. Like Dear-eyes, she walked in a mist. Then Pearl and I came, and her people warned her privately that if she attempted to return with us they would attack us with their iron-shod staves. They brought those staves to that meeting which was so difficult. She dare not take their talk as a mere threat, for some of her clan had attacked even Englishmen — and we were only women — but she dare not tell us their purpose.

'You would have laughed at their threats. I dared not come with you lest they should attack you on the way to the cart or on the lonely road. So I saw you off in silence, despairing of deliverance.'

And then, to her deeper despair, she was hurried through a marriage 'to bind her to her people for ever'. But little comforters were given to her — two little daughters so fair and beautiful that people called them children of heaven. 'And to heaven they went, one when she was three and the other before she was two. I had taught them to love the Name of our Lord Jesus, and I longed that they should be signed with His Sign; but there was no one to do it. So when I saw that He was about to take my little Queen, I myself dipped my hand in water, and I marked her with His Sign, and she looked up and all around the room with smiling eyes, and I thought, Surely she is seeing Him and His angels. And I looked to Him whom I did not see, and I said, "Take her," and He took her.

'Then Death came running quickly and caught the younger one. I had no time to go for fresh water, but near me was some rice-water in a bowl, and I signed her with His Sign, using the rice-water, and I gave her to Him too. And He took her. Afterwards I thanked Him. I said, "They could not have grown up good in this hell. O my Lord, I am glad they are safe in Thy Country." So saying I was comforted; and both my babies were far more beautiful in death than ever they had been in life.'

It was a Sunday evening when she told us this. 'I have just come back from the House of Prayer; I saw a wonderful thing,' she said — 'I saw Godfrey Annachie burn magical palm-leaf books and other things that a converted magician had given him. He put them on a great tray and poured oil on them, and the flames shot up, and we sang and sang. For twelve years I never once sang aloud, only in my heart I sang the old songs, but never aloud. It was like a dream, like the dream that I

116

dreamt so often. I used to be sure I was home, and then I woke up and wept to find it was only a dream.'

Will this reach one who had waited fifteen years for a Dear-eyes or twelve years for a Tranquillity — perhaps longer? We waited twenty-four for our Mimosa. In the end — O troubled heart, believe it — Love will find a way. Your sorrow shall be turned into joy. *If any of thine be driven out unto the outmost parts of heaven, from thence will the Lord thy God gather thee, and from thence will He fetch thee.* Let us be confident, then, and sing before we see, and trust our unconquerable Lord, whose words stand deep-rooted like the rocks of the mountains.

> Our human hope, it waxeth but to wane,
> Hope faileth not that of Thy love is born;
> Make hope our habit; blessed love constrain,
> Till flowers shall bloom where now is only thorn.

W 118

## Casting our care on the Lord

The hills of Southern India drop steeply towards the Indian Ocean. From the high rocks where the ibex find safe foothold you can see the waves that continually wash up in vast quantities two kinds of magnetic sand, monazite and ilmenite. Monazite is composed largely of thorium (the name looks back to the Scandinavian Thor) and is used in making incandescent gas mantles. It glistens, but is of a dull colour. The pure thorium oxide is extracted from ilmenite and is used as the finest pigment in white paint and enamel. Ilmenite is black. The valuable sand is separated from the other sand (which looks far more valuable, for it often seems all garnet and crystal and jacinth) first by magnet, and finally by vibrating tables down which it is run, and where the magnetic impurities are separated out by gravity.

The process of water-grinding in the sea (by which the particles of ore are detached from the original rock), friction of grain upon grain in the rough and tumble of the waves, the influence of a force which we name and use but cannot explain, the tedious, tiny agitations of the vibrating tables, which call into effective co-operation the mighty pull of the earth — all these processes work together to bring forth from a black sand whiteness, and from a dull-coloured sand a substance which helps towards illumination.

And the first of these is the breaking up of the rock in the bed of the sea; the discipline of renunciation. It is a figure of the true. First the severance: that which is death to the old order of being, then many a blow that we call blinding, little unexplained constraints, tedious minutes of shifting circumstance — that out of mere dust of earth something good may be prepared for the use of Him whom we call Master and Lord.

And all this is part of the preparation for the spiritual climb.

It is true that 'for a man never to feel trouble, nor suffer none heaviness in body nor in soul, is not the state of this world, but the state of everlasting quiet,' and yet it is possible to cast all our care on our Lord or we should not be told to do so. And sometimes the cares are so many and so heavy that if we did not cast them we could not bear up at all. The one way, then, is the old way — Casting all your care upon Him for He careth for you.

GM 64

### A letter to one in need

Are you getting plenty of quiet with God? Remember the words I so often quote from Jeanne De Chantal. 'We cannot measure the love He showers on souls who give and abandon themselves to Him, and who have no higher aspiration than to do all that they believe to be pleasing to Him.' If only we live so, then there can be nothing to fear; we shall radiate peace and joy and love, and the shout of a King will be ever among us.

You often remind me of myself. Too much of your nature is exposed to the winds that blow upon it. You and I both need to withdraw more and more into the secret place with God. Do you know what I mean, I wonder?

CD 111

### Consolation

We have a very understanding Master: we have noticed that when some specially sharp strain on faith and hope and patience is to follow, then He draws near beforehand, and with shining wings overshadows us, and there is a sound of gentle stillness, there is speech. Or there may be a Showing (I think this word must be the right one, for long before I met it in old books it was the only one that came to express the luminous thing that

119

I mean). And through the hours or even years that come after, before there is fulfilment, the soul that heard, that saw, knows only to say to itself and to all that confronts it, *I believe God that it shall be even as it was told me.* What a Lord is ours — 'Many a visit does He make to the interior man, sweet is His communication with him, delightful is His consolation, great is His peace, and His familiarity exceedingly amazing.'

GC 183

## *Mountains*

DEUTERONOMY 2.3.    *Ye have compassed this mountain long enough.*

There is a mountain which, when I find myself compassing it, I call by this name, Discontent with the ways of God. It has other names which sound nicer, but I think this name strips it of all pretence.

How can we know if we are compassing that mountain? Do we fit anywhere into this sentence from the *Imitation?* 'Many privily seek themselves in things that they do, and wot not thereof. It seemeth them also that they stand in their good peace when all things fall after their will and their feeling. And if it fall otherwise than they desire, they are soon moved and sorry.' If we find ourselves there, then we may know that we are compassing that mountain. But we need not compass it for one hour longer. 'Ye have compassed this mountain long enough.' It is a trumpet-note word. We are called to be soldiers. Soldiers obey the call of the trumpet. Let us obey.

EW 80

120

## Meditation

There is a way into the greenwood which is not much used in these days of feverish rush. Its name in the Scriptures is Meditation. ('Let my meditation be sweet unto Him.') We should plough a deeper furrow if we knew more of that way. We should be quieter then, and there is nothing creative in noise. 'Friend, when dost thou *think?*' asked the old Quaker after listening to a modern time-table; we cannot think by machinery. We cannot consider the lilies without giving time to the lilies. Often our flash of haste means little. To read a book in an hour (if the book has taken half a life-time to write) means nothing at all. To pray in a hurry of spirit means nothing. To live in a hurry means to do much but effect little. We build more quickly in wood, hay, and stubble than in gold, silver, precious stones; but the one abides, the other does not.

If he who feels the world is too much with him will make for himself a little space, and let his mind settle like a bee in a flower on some great word of his God, and brood over it, pondering it till it has time to work in him, he will find himself in the greenwood.

GM 111

## Distractions

Often, when we are most in earnest to pray, we are tormented by wandering thoughts and distractions of all sorts. I have been reading some old books lately and find that exactly the same thing distressed others. 'The noise of a fly', as one says, is enough to distract him. Do not fuss, do not worry, do not spend time wondering why that thought came just then or that other interruption was allowed (for that is playing into the enemy's hands); but as soon as you are conscious that you have been drawn away, peacefully come back again. 'Return unto thy rest, O my soul.'

Faber describes these uncomfortable things as 'unmannerly distractions [which] come and force my thoughts from Thee.'

There will be times when we forget ourselves and everyone else and everything else, and are caught up, absorbed; there is no word for what this is. But it will not be so every day. There must be something salutary in the pressing through which prayer generally means. 'When Thou saidst, Seek ye My face; my heart said unto Thee, Thy face, Lord, will I seek.' There is a seeking; there is no seeing without that seeking. So the best way is to refuse to be entangled and worried and fussed, and as simply as a child would turn to one whom it loves, so turn to Him whom our soul loveth and, distractions or no distractions, say to Him, 'Thy face, Lord, will I seek.'

EW 89

## Note on prayer and fasting

[*Written for a special week of prayer*]

This note is to those to whom the idea of 'prayer and fasting' is new, and who are rather puzzled about it.

First, what does it mean?

It means a determined effort to put first things first, even at the cost of some inconvenience to oneself. It means a setting of the will towards God. It means shutting out as much as possible all interrupting things. For the thing that matters is that one cares enough to have time with God, and to say *no* to that in oneself which clamours for a good meal and perhaps conversation. It is *that* which is of value to our Lord. Such a setting of the will Godward is never a vain thing. 'I said not unto the seed of Jacob, Seek ye Me in vain.'

But we must be in earnest. 'When Thou saidst, Seek ye My face; my heart said unto Thee, Thy face, Lord, will I seek.'

A few simple *Dont's*:

1   *Don't* get into bondage about place, or position of the body. Where did our Lord spend His hours of prayer? We know how crowded and stuffy Eastern houses are; we know that sometimes, at least, He went out into the open air to a hillside; to a garden. Where did Elijah spend the long time of waiting on his God? Again, out in the open air. I have known some who could kneel for hours by a chair. I have known others who could not. David 'sat before the Lord'. Some find help in going out of doors and walking up and down; this was Bishop Moule's way. Some go into their room and shut their door. Do not be in bondage. Let the leaning of your mind lead you; a God-directed mind leans to what helps the spirit most.

2   *Don't* be discouraged if at first you seem to get nowhere. I think there is no command in the whole Bible so difficult to

obey and so penetrating in power, as the command to be still —
'Be still, and know that I am God'. Many have found this so.

> Ah dearest Lord! I cannot pray,
>     My fancy is not free;
> Unmannerly distractions come,
>     And force my thoughts from Thee.
>
> The world that looks so dull all day
>     Glows bright on me at prayer,
> And plans that ask no thought but then
>     Wake up and meet me there.
>
> All nature one full fountain seems
>     Of dreamy sight and sound,
> Which, when I kneel, breaks up its deeps,
>     And makes a deluge round.
>
> My very flesh has restless fits;
>     My changeful limbs conspire
> With all these phantoms of the mind
>     My inner self to tire.

Faber

This is true. Let the tender understanding of your God
enfold you. He knows the desire of your heart. Sooner or later
He will fulfill it. It is written, 'He will fulfil the desire of them
that fear Him'. 'I said not unto the seed of Jacob, Seek ye Me in
vain.' (Thank God, for using the poor name *Jacob* there. Do
you not often feel very much like the seed of Jacob? I do.
'Surely, shall one say, In the Lord have I righteousness and
strength.' There is none of either in the seed of Jacob).

3   *Don't* feel it necessary to pray all the time; listen. Solomon
asked for a hearing heart. It may be that the Lord wants to
search the ground of your heart, not the top layer, but the

ground. Give Him time to do this. And read the Words of Life. Let them enter into you.

4  *Don't* forget there is one other person interested in you — extremely interested; he will talk, probably quite vehemently, for there is no truer word than the old couplet,

> Satan trembles when he sees
> The weakest saint upon his knees.

As far as I know the only way to silence his talk is to read or say aloud (or recall to mind) counter-words, 'It is written . . . It is written . . . It is written'; or to sing, for the devil detests song. 'Singing . . . in your heart', 'singing . . . to the Lord' — either or both are too much for him.

But let the Spirit lead as to what to read. 'Let Thy loving Spirit lead me forth into the land of righteousness.'

5  *Don't* give up in despair if no thoughts and no words come, but only distractions and inward confusions. Often it helps to use the words of others, making them one's own. Psalm, hymn, song — use what helps most.

6  *Don't* worry if you fall asleep. 'He giveth unto His beloved in sleep.'

7  And if the day ends in what seems failure, *don't* fret. Tell Him about it. Tell Him you are sorry. Even so, don't be discouraged. All discouragement is of the devil. It is true as Faber says again:

> Had I, dear Lord, no pleasure found
>   But in the thought of Thee,
> Prayer would have come unsought, and been
>   A truer liberty.

Yet Thou art oft most present, Lord,
  In weak distracted prayer;
A sinner out of heart with self
  Most often finds Thee there.

For prayer that humbles sets the soul
  From all illusions free,
And teaches it how utterly,
  Dear Lord, it hangs on Thee.

Then let your soul hang on Him. 'My soul hangeth upon Thee' — not upon my happiness in prayer, but just upon Thee. Tell Him you are sorry, and fall back on the old words: 'Lord, Thou knowest all things; Thou knowest that I love Thee' — unworthy as I am. Let these words comfort your heart: 'The Lord . . . lifteth up all those that are down.' 'Cast not away . . . your confidence', there is a 'great recompense of reward' waiting for you a little later on.

But maybe it will be quite different. 'Sometimes a light surprises the Christian when he sings', or waits with his heart set upon access to his God; and he is bathed in wonder that to such dust of the earth such revelations of love can be given. If so it be, to Him be the praise. It is all of Him.

*'Now the God of peace, that brought again from the dead our Lord Jesus, that great Shepherd of the sheep, through the blood of the everlasting covenant, make you perfect in every good work to do His will, working in you that which is well-pleasing in His sight, through Jesus Christ; to whom be glory for ever and ever. Amen.'*

EW 194

## The cross

**LUKE** 9.23. *If any man will come after Me, let him deny himself, and take up his cross daily and follow Me.*

I think often we accept the cross in theory, but when it comes to practice, we either do not recognize it for what it is, or we recognize it and try to avoid it. This we can always do, for the cross is something that can be taken up or left, just as we choose. It is *not* illness (that comes to all), or bereavement (that also is the common lot of man). It is something *voluntarily* suffered for the sake of the Lord Jesus, some denial of self, that would not be if we were not following Him; often it is something that has shame in it (this, of course, was the earliest connotation of the word), such as the misunderstanding of friends and their blame, when the principles which govern our lives appear foolishness to them. It always has at its core the denial of self and self-love in all its manifestation. Self-choices go down before the call to take up the cross and follow. They fade away and cease to be.

EW 52

**GALATIANS** 2.20. (Weymouth) *I have been crucified with Christ, and it is no longer I that live, but Christ that lives in me.*

Just when we most earnestly desire to live like this, the weary old self seems to come to life again — the 'I' that we had trusted was crucified with Christ. It is very disappointing when this happens, and the devil watches not far away, and very quietly and with great subtlety he tries to draw us into hopeless distress and despair. If he can do that he is satisfied, for then we are occupied with ourselves, which is what he wants us to be.

The one and only thing is to look straight off ourselves and our wretched failure, and cry to Him who is mighty to save. He never refuses that cry; so do not fear. The moment self is recognized, look to Him. Do not be discouraged; He is not discouraged. He who has begun a good work in us will go on to perfect it. The going on may take time; even so, He will go on till (O blessed 'till') we are perfected.

EW 53

## Peace

COLOSSIANS 3.15.  *Let the peace of God rule in your hearts.*

If we open the shutters in the morning the light will pour in. We do not need to beseech it to pour in. It will pour in if we will let it. If we open the sluice in flood-time the water will flow through. We do not plead with it to flow. It will flow if we will let it.

It is so with the peace of God. It will rule in our hearts if only we will let it. If a heart that is disturbed about anything will 'let the peace of God rule' (instead of its own desires), that heart may this very day prove this truth.

*Let not your heart be troubled:*
*Let the peace of God rule in your hearts.*  (John 14.1)

EW 67

## Power

PSALM 119.173.  *Let Thine hand help me.*

This little prayer has often been mine. These short Bible prayers are just what we want in days when we are tired or hard-pressed, so I pass this one on for those who need it. You will find it enough. It is like the touch on the electric light switch — just a touch, and the power comes flowing from the power-house — the power that turns to light.

EW 149

128

## Find harbour

I understand the buffetted days and the days of no small tempest, when neither sun nor stars appear. And it is good to pass through such days, for if we didn't we could neither prove our God nor help others. If any experience of ours helps to bring others to our Lord, what does any buffetting matter?

But we are not meant to live in a perpetual stormy sea. We are meant to pass through and find harbour and so be at peace. Then we are free from occupation with ourselves and our storms — free to help others.

I want to live in the light of the thought of His coming, His triumph — the end of this present darkness, the glory of His seen Presence. This bathes the present in radiance. You won't be sorry then that you trusted when you couldn't see, when neither sun nor stars in many days appeared and no small tempest lay on you (Acts 27.20). No, you won't be sorry then. So I won't be sorry now. I am believing. 'All joy and peace in believing': the words ring like a chime of bells.

CD 64

## One of the secrets of happiness

One of the great secrets of happiness is to think of happy things. There were many unhappy things in Philippi, things false, dishonourable, unjust, impure, hideous and of very bad report; the air of Philippi was darkened by these things. The Christians of that town might easily have had their lives stained by continually letting their thoughts dwell on what they could not help seeing and hearing and feeling, the evil which they must often have met and fought in their striving together for the faith of the Gospel. But they were definitely told to think of things true, honourable, just, pure, lovely and of good report. 'And if there be any virtue, and if there be any praise, think on these things.'

GM 46

## Moss

We are too high; Lord Jesus, we implore Thee,
  Make of us something like the low green moss,
That vaunteth not, a quiet thing before Thee,
  Cool for Thy feet sore wounded on the Cross.

Like low, green moss—and yet our thoughts are thronging,
  Running to meet Thee, all alight, afire;
Thirsty the soul that burneth in love-longing
  Fountain and fire art Thou, and heart's desire.

Therefore we come, Thy righteousness our cover,
  Thy precious Blood our one, our only plea,
Therefore we come, O Saviour, Master, Lover.
  To whom, Lord, could we come save unto Thee?

TJ 76

# 4

## Words of Wisdom

Certain it is that the reason there is so much shallow living, much talk, but little obedience, is that so few are prepared to be, like the pine on the hill-top, alone in the wind for God.

GM 160

'I will show him what great things he must suffer for My sake' — not what great things he must do, achieve, enjoy.   GM 161

What the ground offers to the corn of wheat is not the rapture of welcome, but only a quiet place into which it may fall and die.                                                    WT 181

No master is responsible for uncommanded work.     GC 125

True valour lies, not in what the world calls success, but in the dogged going on when everything in the man says Stop. RB 66

Will-power fails under certain forms of trial long continued.

P 6

'I do not want people who come to me under certain reservations. In battle you need soldiers who fear nothing.' So said Père Didon; so say I.                              P 44

The Indian mind is made of folds, firmly folded in unexpected places.                                                            P 66

You cannot pull people uphill who do not want to go; you can only point up.                                                    P 74

There have been times of late when I have had to hold on to one text with all my might. 'It is required in stewards that a man be found *faithful*.' Praise God, it does not say 'successful'.

TTA 18

Nothing is hopeless to God; 'Set no borders to His strength,' a Japanese missionary said. We say it over and over again to ourselves, in the face of some great hopelessness.     TTA 28

We find that if the soul is to resist the tremendous opposing forces which will instantly be brought to bear upon it if it turns in the least towards Christ, there must be a *conviction* wrought within it; nothing so superficial as a *feeling*, be it ever so appreciative or hopeful or loving, will stand that strain.

TTA 61

Fear can hamstring the soul.     GC 43

It is God's truth that one loving spirit sets others on fire.

GC 66

More and more I feel that love is the golden secret of life. The very air of heaven is love, for God is love and love never fails. So go on loving not only the loveless but the unloveable, the difficult, the perplexing, the disappointing — unto the end.

CD 99

It is never safe for a convert, or for a child who is practically a convert, to be unhappy for long. Behind him or her is a darkness. Phantoms haunt that darkness, and memories, like hands, are ever pulling, pulling, pulling.     GC 152

Ragland's happiness, so evidently not caused by circumstances, but by something invisible and abiding, affected the people . . . for it impinged upon an existence bounded for the most part by fear pushed far into the background of consciousness, but always there, in spite of periods of gay excitement. And except the mysterious aloofness of asceticism, nothing is so attractive in India as supernaturally sustained happiness.     RSP 70

There is a Tamil word for insincerity which means literally *showing brass for gold.*                                              GC 165

Endure in your own flesh for a while the sharpness of acute, unrelieved pain, and you know how divine a thing the touch of the healer is.                                              GC 291

My flesh and my heart faileth — let them fail. For God is the strength of my heart, and my portion for ever. Has anyone ever been able to tell what our glorious Lord can be to man, woman or little child whom He is training to wait upon Him only?

GC 62

We say, then, to anyone who is under trial, give Him time to steep the soul in His eternal truth. Go into the open air, look up into the depths of the sky, or out upon the wideness of the sea, or on the strength of the hills that is His also; or, if bound in the body, go forth in the spirit; spirit is not bound. Give Him time and, as surely as dawn follows night, there will break upon the heart a sense of certainty that cannot be shaken.

GC 125

# Books by Amy Carmichael

Amy Carmichael of Dohnavur ......... Biography by Frank L. Houghton
Candles in the Dark ....................................... Letters of counsel
Edges of His Ways ......................................... Daily devotional
Figures of the True ..................................... Readings with photographs
God's Missionary ................................... Booklet on being a missionary
Gold by Moonlight ...................... Thoughts by A.C. with photographs
Gold Cord .................................. The story of *The Dohnavur Fellowship*
His Thoughts Said . . . His Father Said . . . ...................... Short readings
If ....................................... Challenging free verse beginning with *"If"*
Learning of God ............................................ Selected prose and poetry
Mimosa .............................................. A true story of an Indian woman
Mountain Breezes ........................................ Anthology of A.C.'s poetry
Rose From Brier .................................. Devotional, especially for the ill
Thou Givest . . . They Gather ..................................... Topical devotional
Toward Jerusalem ............................................. Selected poetry
Whispers of His Power .................................... Daily devotional

These books are available at your local bookstore or write, fax or e-mail:

CHRISTIAN ✦ LITERATURE ✦ CRUSADE
Box 1449, Fort Washington, PA 19034
Fax: 1-215-542-7580 • E-mail: CLCBOOKS@juno.com